PUTTING THE PROSPERITY IDEA

TO WORK

A Companion Volume

to

You, Too, Can Be Prosperous

By

Robert Russell

CONTENTS

Introduction.. 1

1. Prosperity and the Absolute 5

2. Prosperity and Business 9

3. Prosperity and Business Attitudes 11

4. Prosperity and Compensations............................ 15

5. Prosperity and Confidence.................................. 17

6. Prosperity and Credit 19

7. Prosperity and Debts... 23

8. Prosperity and Debtors.. 25

9. Prosperity and Desire.. 27

10. Prosperity and Discouragement 31

11. Prosperity and Employment............................... 35

12. Prosperity and Faultfinding................................ 39

13. Prosperity and Fear 43

14. Prosperity and Financial Reverses 47

15. Prosperity and Forgiveness 51

16. Prosperity and Giving 53

17. Prosperity and Giving Cheerfully 55

18. Prosperity and Human Thought......................... 57

19. Prosperity and Imagination 59

20. Prosperity and Just Return (Law of Non-Possession)...... 63

21. Prosperity and the Kingdom (Investments) 67

22. Prosperity and the Law 71

23. Prosperity and the Magnet (Law of Attraction)............... 75

24. Prosperity and Negative Thought   77

25. Prosperity and Obedience   81

26. Prosperity and Praise – I   85

27. Prosperity and Praise – II   89

28. Prosperity and Property   93

29. Prosperity and Your Queries   97

30. Prosperity and Resentment   103

31. Prosperity and Saving   107

32. Prosperity and Security   111

33. Prosperity and Self-Faith   115

34. Prosperity and Sorrow   119

35. Prosperity and Stewardship   123

36. Prosperity and Strain   127

37. Prosperity and Supply   131

38. Prosperity and Taxes   135

39. Prosperity and Thanksgiving   137

40. Prosperity and Tithing   141

41. Prosperity and Understanding   145

42. Prosperity and Values – I (Deceitfulness of Riches)   149

43. Prosperity and Values – II   153

44. Prosperity and Worry   157

45. Prosperity and Xmas (Christmas)   161

46. Prosperity and You   165

47. Prosperity and Zeal   169

FOREWORD

This book is practical, not theoretical. It is intended for those who wish to go all the way in demonstrating the Law. It is for those who are willing to take the ideas presented here on faith and put them to work in their lives. It is assumed that the reader will not only read, mark, learn, and inwardly digest these statements but that he will prove them by acting upon them with faith and confidence. Prosperity is an exact science, and to approach it in the right way is to succeed. To approach it in the wrong way is to fail.

There is a sequence to be followed in demonstrating prosperity. "Order is Heaven's first Law." We must put first things first. If we get the fundamentals right, the superstructure will be right. It is important at the beginning of a study of this kind to understand not only the ways in which supply moves but our part in keeping it moving; in other words, to know how to keep the idea whirling on its axis once it has begun to revolve.

Many people think that prosperity depends upon outer circumstances and conditions – a particular job, profession, position, or business, but that is not true. Prosperity is a state of Consciousness, and anyone who has the Consciousness will demonstrate prosperity no matter where he is. It is not the job or business that makes a man prosperous but what he brings to it. The whole matter turns on Consciousness; without the

Consciousness of success and prosperity, the finest business produces very little.

The Law of Giving and Receiving (which is the Law of Prosperity) is infallible. The way to prove it is for you to specialize it for your good. *"Look unto me and be ye saved all the ends of the earth."* No one who looks to God for his supply can fail to be prosperous.

"Faith without works is dead." So is knowledge without action. Live with this book until you have embodied the principles contained in it. You will know without question when the book has served its purpose for you by the changed conditions in your life.

Robert A. Russell

INTRODUCTION

What you get out of this book will be determined by what you put into it and whether you read it in the letter or in the spirit. The blessing of good that you are seeking is seeking you. It is right where you are, awaiting your recognition and acceptance. Yes, I know that you have tried to demonstrate health, success, prosperity, and freedom, and feel that you have failed. Perhaps you have tried to use the Power instead of moving with it. You may have tried to personalize it with the human mind instead of letting It come to you through the Christ Mind. Here is a fresh start. By the very act of reading this page, you prove that you recognize your need. Along with that recognition, take two short verses from the New Testament into your Consciousness and make them a part of your basic thinking: *"Your Father knoweth what things ye have need of before ye ask him"* and *"Son, thou art ever with me, and all that I have is thine."*

The treadmill of your thought probably runs like this: *Things are going down again. Jobs are harder to get. We're facing another depression. Money is tight. Money is hard to get. "The old gray mare ain't what she used to be."* Why are you outlining? Why are you making evil patterns for yourself? Why are you speculating? Why are you trying to find a way to get the things which you already have? Why do you need a rope and bucket for the things that are yours merely for the acceptance?

You recall the woman by the well of Sychar to whom Jesus offered living water (Life Eternal). She could not take it because the well was deep and because she had no comprehension of what He was talking about. She was more interested in the depth of the well and in the reason for his conversation. You remember that he was a Jew and she a Samaritan. "How did I know it was Jesus?" she probably said later to her friends. "I had never seen Him before, and it could have been a highwayman." Of course, she couldn't know Him; she was more interested in the personality of the speaker than in His gift. She wanted to know if Jesus was greater than Abraham; she wanted to know how you could draw water without a bucket and a rope.

"The woman saith unto Him, Sir, Thou hast nothing to draw with, and the well is deep: from whence hast Thou that living water?

Jesus answered and said unto her, Whosoever drinketh of this water shall thirst again:

But whosoever drinketh of the water that I shall give him shall never thirst; but the water that I shall give him shall be in him a well of water springing into everlasting life."

Man often fails to realize his blessings because he is more interested in the process involved than in the gift itself. He must take in all the lectures, go to all the churches, get all the interpretations, and buy all the courses; he instinctively senses that the gift is there, but thinks he must go around his thumb to get it. He does not realize that *"The wisdom of this world is foolishness with God."* He must have a bucket and a rope. He must figure out how his supply will get to him and from whom it will come. He must outline. He must measure the depth of the well and know all about the differences in nationalities. Jesus says, *"All things are yours."* But He is not offering you things that must be hammered out of steel, molded out of clay, carved out of wood, or fashioned by human hands. He is offering you things that must be delivered in their own way. Your part is not to chisel them out of concrete but to appropriate them through a new Consciousness. It is the same Consciousness that enabled the beggar at the temple gate to jump up and run.

1. PROSPERITY AND THE ABSOLUTE

"I MYSELF AM GOOD FORTUNE."

The most direct approach to prosperity is through the Absolute. We say direct approach because the Absolute scientist makes no concession to lack or want in any form. He proves God and his Consciousness to be one and includes himself within the whole. If it is true of God, it must be true in manifestation: this statement is the position of the Absolute scientist. All his demonstrations are made from that standpoint. God is all in all. He is both desire and fulfillment, prayer and its answer, idea and its manifestation. There is but One Mind; your mind and my mind are in it and of it; therefore, all visible manifestations are under the dominion of our mind.

This is the highest form of practice. It is not a system or process but a way of thinking. The principle of the Absolutist is Absolute Oneness with God. He is our own Consciousness – "closer is He than breathing and nearer than hands and feet." When we glimpse this Oneness, we shall stop trying to demonstrate money and start demonstrating the Substance of our own Consciousness.

The Absolute scientist, according to Vivian May Williams, works on the assumption that "we cannot possess money until we perceive that the substance of our own form or identity is the same substance or wealth of which money is the identity. If you believe that you are spiritual and money is material, you separate yourself from it by accepting such a belief. But when you realize that money is a spiritual idea that stands in the same relationship to Mind, God, as a rose does, it will be visibly expressed without anxious thought."

Working in the Absolute is an awakening rather than a process. Before you can work successfully, you must not only be able to disregard appearances but you must learn to work with facts. The statement of St. John is very definite: *"I know thy works and tribulations, and poverty, but thou art rich."* To all appearances you are troubled and in want, but back of the appearance is the fact – YOU ARE RICH.

We talk of supply as though it were the cause of such things as money, houses, automobiles, radios; these are not causes but effects. The real cause of material blessings is in the Law of Consciousness. Before one can individualize (use) the Law of Consciousness, he must become aware of it. Jesus said, *"Seek ye first the Kingdom of God."* Seek first an awareness of this Law as your supply. When you have it, *"all these things shall be added unto you."* There will be no limit to your supply because there is no limit to your Consciousness.

The only thing we ever suffer from is lack of awareness. The only thing that limits us is a thought of limitation. If we are to get above limitation, we must live and think on a higher plane of Consciousness. We must train ourselves to believe that nothing in the outer world can affect us or be a law unto us.

The Absolutist knows only the present tense, for the only time in the Absolute is NOW. If God *is*, prosperity *is*. If God *is* in instant manifestation, prosperity *is* in instant manifestation. But we must become conscious or aware of the fact before it has any significance in our lives.

What is it you are seeking to demonstrate? Is it a job? Is it a car? A home? Is it health? Realize that you have no capacity to create or to engender anything; your only capacity is to become aware, or to accept. What you are seeking is seeking you. IT IS HERE NOW. It is already in manifestation. It is already established. Await its materialization with joyful expectation.

"NOW IS THE ACCEPTED TIME."

2. PROSPERITY AND BUSINESS

The motto for the successful business man was given to us by St. Paul: *"Be not slothful in business; [be] fervent in spirit; serving the Lord."* It makes no difference whether our business is directing a bank, making a home, pounding a typewriter, clerking in a store, running a factory, driving a truck, supervising a department, or managing a sales crew, the secret of success in our activity is to bring it into conformity with the Divine Plan. Men used to scoff at this idea. "You can't mix religion and business," they said. "Business is business. You can't bring the Bible precepts into your counting house or factory." But religion has come into business to stay. Men everywhere are finding that their greatest prosperity and their greatest joy in business come from the Practice of the Presence of God. The modern business man is discovering that by the right use of Spiritual Law, he can make himself a magnet to attract all that is desirable. He does not go down with hard times and depressions, but keeps his mind pointed toward his goal. Knowing that he is one with God, he knows that he cannot fail.

The two kinds of business men set forth in our motto are the slothful (inactive) man and the God-centered (active) man. The one serves self; the other serves the Lord. The one thinks down; the other thinks up. Let us get a clear picture of these two types. The slothful business man sits idly by waiting for things to happen. He is satisfied with old methods, old ideas, old equipment, old associations, and old environment. He lives in the past and dreads change in any form. He is like water that is allowed to rest. You recall that it soon becomes stagnant.

The God-centered man, on the other hand, not only thinks up but is up and doing. He does not think of his business as his own but as God's. He sees every line of activity in the business world as part of the One Activity. He does not complain about competition, monopoly, overhead, scarcity, and contingencies because he knows that cycles of prosperity and depression are brought about by men's thoughts and expectations.

Conditions never rise any higher than our thought standards. If we face toward failure and ruin, we cannot expect to be successful and prosperous. If we are always complaining, griping, and talking our business down, we produce a pattern that the mind will follow and materialize. The God-centered man will not only hold the right attitude toward his business, but will hustle to make his dream come true.

"I AND MY FATHER ARE ONE."

3. PROSPERITY AND BUSINESS ATTITUDES

"AS A MAN THINKETH IN HIS HEART, SO IS HE."

In the past, man depended largely upon his hands and personal effort to make his living. He worked out his finances very painfully and used subtle devices of cunning. grasping, and outwitting his neighbor. Today practical religion has placed in man's hands a better and more fitting means of securing a livelihood. The old idea was that man should earn his living by the sweat of his brow, by struggle and hard labor; the Christ way is by indirection or laborless activity. *"Seek ye first the Kingdom of God and His righteousness* [right mindedness]," said Jesus, *"and all these things shall be added unto you."* This promise does not mean that man has no work to do on the physical plane but means that he must do his work in the right spirit. If faith without works is dead, so is thought without action.

Let us get on with the subject of mental attitudes. What is a mental attitude? A mental attitude is the sum total of one's thoughts, beliefs, convictions, expectations, and feelings. The habitual attitude not only determines a man's character but what he attracts from the outside world. We think of it as a magnet that attracts the people, opportunities, circumstances, and things that are in harmony with it. It is most important, therefore, that we develop the kind of mental attitude that will attract the things that we want.

The psychiatrist concerns himself with many attitudes; the metaphysician concerns himself with only two – the positive and the negative. The positive attitude sees things in their relation to God; the negative attitude sees things in their relation to self. The positive attitude expects and attracts the good and desirable things of life; the negative attitude expects and attracts the evil and undesirable things. Our mental attitudes are vitally important in the business of living and demonstrating because they interpret us to others. "Like attracts like." "Birds of a feather flock together." If we go about with the mental attitude of defeat, fear, worry, frustration, and confusion, others will tune into our adverse mental states and govern themselves toward us accordingly. They will be attracted or repelled by the prevailing mental state which we hold. Emerson said, "What you are screams so loud that I cannot hear what you say." What you are is what you are attracting from the world.

You think this is a lot of nonsense, do you? Then make a careful study of any rich man you know, and see if his prevailing mental state is not one of opulence and plenty. It never dawns on him that he could ever be impoverished or poor. He builds the opposite idea into his mental attitude and is constantly supported by it; he lives with the expectation of prosperity. The positive man does not take his business to bed with him and worry half the night. He does not go to pieces over breakage, spoilage, and the mistakes of his employees.

He does not poison his brain with fear, anger, or temper. He knows that negative attitudes not only sap his vitality and defeat his purpose but invite disaster.

Begin this very moment to establish in your mental attitudes those things which you wish to attract. Set up a new ideal of financial success, and hold the creative thought that everything good is being attracted to you now. See it, feel it, demand it, and accept it.

I AM PROSPERED BY THE INCREASING MULTIPLYING POWER OF GOD SUBSTANCE.

4. PROSPERITY AND COMPENSATIONS

"THE LABORER IS WORTHY OF HIS HIRE."

While we are on the subject of giving and receiving, it might be helpful to say a word about right compensation for spiritual work. Most people treat this matter casually when actually one of the basic rules for keeping the demonstration alive and for preserving the contact between Cause and Effect is involved. "The Law," as E. V. Ingraham says, "perpetuates and amplifies whatever it is allowed to act upon. Giving preserves this contact. It keeps your affairs in contact with Creative Power. The fruits of the law are contingent upon observance of the Law."

A consecrated minister, healer, or practitioner has no desire to capitalize on his ministry but only to be supported while he gives generously of his knowledge and of his time. He knows, or should know, how to demonstrate his own supply, but there is another side to the Law. That is the client's side. A true spiritual healer knows that the client can receive no benefits from metaphysical treatments until he fulfills his part of the Law. If he is seeking healing and does not support the practitioner who labors for him, he will not be healed.

The law of compensation was clearly stated by Jesus: *"Whatsoever a man soweth, that shall he also reap." "With what measure ye mete, it shall be measured to you again." "Give, and it shall be given unto you."* You must compensate your minister or practitioner, not because he demands it or expects it, but because compensation is an integral part of the process of receiving. This obligation exists not only for personal counseling and treatments, but for funerals, baptisms, weddings, and other ministrations as well. If you accept the time and services of anyone without making a fair and just return, you not only break the law but you set up a debit against yourself in the ledger of life. You create a gap in Consciousness (a sense of guilt) that will hinder any future demonstrations of good.

The reason Jesus laid so much stress on giving is that giving enlarges the capacity for receiving. If you wish to be healed and to stay healed, pay your practitioner according to the benefits you expect to receive.

BY COMPENSATING GENEROUSLY FOR ANY SERVICE, I ESTABLISH A RECIPROCAL ACTION BETWEEN THE UNIVERSE AND MY BUSINESS AND FINANCES.

5. Prosperity and Confidence

"IN THEE IS MY TRUST."

When you go to a store and buy a piano, radio, washing machine, or groceries and have them charged to your account, that is called credit – from the Latin word, *credo* (I believe). Your dealer lets you have the things you want because he has faith that you will pay your bill when it is due. Confidence comes from the Latin word, *confido* (I trust). Faith and trust are the basis of all trade. Business is good or bad according to the confidence we have in one another.

"Some people," says Edward Beals in his booklet, *The Law of Financial Success,* "seem to be of a naturally suspicious frame of mind, always of the opinion that somebody else is trying to 'do' them. Others are gullible and swallow everything – bait, hook, and line. Neither is the wisest frame of mind. It is much better to maintain the thought of good will, fellowship, and confidence towards one's fellow man, weighing all things impartially from an unprejudiced standpoint, and then render your decision after due thought from the facts in the case. But by all means have faith in your fellow man." Faith begets faith. If you have faith in your fellow man, he will have faith in you. In faith is faith reflected.

Those who have studied dogs tell us that the canine gets our number at his first scent, that he knows whether we are friendly or fearful on first contact. He gets this information through the atmosphere or vibrations which we emanate. It may not have occurred to you that there is a feeling and appraising sense in man that is akin to the smelling and appraising sense of dogs.

Recall your own dealings, feelings, impulses, and impressions of others, and you will see that there is an even more subtle instinct and judging sense in man. We know that people fall in love at first sight; that some persons always wisely trust their first impressions; that we attract some people and repel others. When we understand that our thinking and feeling create an atmosphere that reveals us to others, we shall be very careful to build into that atmosphere the faith, trust, and love necessary for our highest good. If we are weak, negative, and unbelieving, we surround ourselves with an atmosphere of failure that repels people. If we are strong, positive, and confident, we radiate an atmosphere of success that attracts people. The whole thing simmers down to this: The confidence others have in us depends upon the confidence we have in them. When we combine self-faith and faith in others, we are invincible. The only place in which Jesus could do no mighty works was in His home town. Why? Because of the unbelief – the lack of faith – that prevailed there.

"IF THOU CANST BELIEVE, ALL THINGS ARE POSSIBLE TO HIM THAT BELIEVETH."

6. PROSPERITY AND CREDIT

"HOW MUCH OWEST THOU UNTO MY LORD?"

One of the things that complicate living and retard prosperity is credit. Like money, it can be a blessing or a curse according to the way it is used. If we appreciate the credit system and know how to use it to advantage, it can be a blessing. If we abuse it, it can be a curse.

The lives of many people who buy more than they can pay for bear this out. Possibly the worst thing that can be said about installment plans is that they enslave people and rob them of their contentment, freedom, happiness, and peace.

Easy payment plans that mortgage the pay check for weeks, months, and even years ahead are not *easy* payment plans but *hard* payment plans. There are times when credit is a necessary and good thing, but people who like to buy things with money they do not have give it a bad name. Obligations that cannot be met when due lead to complications, strain, worry, and fear.

The desire to have a beautiful home, attractive furniture, pretty clothes, and fine automobiles is natural and normal. It is right to have them if we can pay for them. It is not right if we have to go into debt and worry until they are paid for. If we borrow or charge our way into prosperity, we have the Principle in reverse. We are living on someone else's money. Do you catch the significance of that? It means that you are in bondage to another's good. If you spend all your time paying for dead horses, you will never get ahead.

False pride or desire to keep up with the Joneses sometimes causes people to do foolish things in order to impress their friends. They sometimes order a beautiful Oriental rug sent out on approval, and after the party send it back to the store. Storekeepers say the same thing is often done with dresses, furniture, and radios. When will we learn that we never cheat anyone but ourselves? We need to stop trying to get something for nothing, to stop trying to be somebody else. Life does not tolerate dishonesty; sometime, somewhere, somehow we pay for everything we get. If it does not come out of our purse, it will come out of our skin, but pay we must.

Success is not measured in terms of fame, fortune, or the abundance of things that a man has, but in terms of integrity, honesty, and the ability to live within one's income. Artificial people build artificial conditions in their bodies and affairs. Happiness is not in having but in being. Peace of mind depends not upon what you spend or do not spend but upon what you think and how you live.

It is always wise, therefore, to buy only what you need and to pay cash for what you get. The stores that have the fewest enemies are those that sell only for cash. They make friends because they help their customers keep their freedom.

"OWE NO MAN ANYTHING, BUT TO LOVE ONE ANOTHER."

7. PROSPERITY AND DEBTS

"BUT IF YE FORGIVE NOT MEN THEIR TRESPASSES, NEITHER WILL YOUR FATHER FORGIVE YOUR TRESPASSES."

In the Lord's Prayer, we are told to pray:

"Forgive us our debts, as we forgive our debtors." You have already met the metaphysical principle involved in this part of the prayer and know that it is impossible to hold two ideas in mind at the same time. Before we can expect forgiveness *(loosen that which is bound* according to the Greek), we must forgive others and forgive ourselves.

Heaven is a state of balance, completeness, happiness, perfection, peace. Debt is a contradiction of the Universal Balance. In reality, there can be no debt because God's Ideas are always complete. If Divine Substance is the common property of all, no thought of debt can enter into it.

Charles Fillmore, in *Prosperity,* says that "Debts exist in the mind, and in the mind is the proper place to begin liquidating them. These thought entities must be abolished in mind before their outer manifestations will pass away and stay away. The world can never be free from the bondage of financial obligations until men erase from their minds the thoughts of 'mine and thine' which generate debts and interest. Analyze the idea of debt and you will see that it involves an idea of lack. Debt is a thought of lack with absence at both ends; the creditor thinks he lacks what is owed him, and the debtor thinks he lacks what is necessary to pay it else he would discharge the obligation rather than continue it. There is error at both ends of the proposition, and nothing in the middle. This being true, it should be easy to dissolve the idea that anyone owes us or that we owe anyone anything. We should fill our mind with thoughts of all-sufficiency, and where there is no lack there can be no debts. Thus we find that the way to pay our debts is by filling our mind with the substance of ideas that are the direct opposite of the ideas of lack that caused the debts."

What we really pray for in this part of the prayer is that we be free of the burden of debt so that we can meet our obligations.

When we get rid of the wrong ideas that produced the debts and substitute the right ideas of abundance and plenty, our debts will be forgiven and paid in full. I *"owe no man anything"* but love. There is magic in these words. If you use them consistently, you will find that you will not only be able to meet all your obligations but that you will help the other fellow to meet his.

I "OWE NO MAN ANYTHING" BUT LOVE.

8. Prosperity and Debtors

MEDITATION

Maude Allison Lathem in *Meditations* phrases a meditation and a treatment that cannot fail to be stimulating.

"The rhythmic circle of Divine Activity is complete in and through me now. Everything coming into me and going out from me is in perfectly balanced, harmonious action. I believe in the Divine promises, and I accept the fact that my word is the scepter of power for me.

"I know that my affairs take on the tone and color of the thoughts that I entertain. It is possible for me to generate a great, creative faith, but I cannot do this while contemplating sin, disease, and disaster. But as my thoughts dwell upon the Spirit incarnated within me, the illumination creates for me a pattern of the highest good. So, no one can decree for me but myself.

"All that is mine comes to me now perfectly, under an exact and divine law."

INDIVIDUAL TREATMENT

"I now declare that no one owes me anything. I bless him whom I have thought of as my debtor, and I know that the God within him makes it possible for him to prosper in all his affairs. Only as my debtor prospers can he carry out his desire to recompense me. Thus I set in motion in a perfectly natural manner the law that brings my own to me.

"I refuse to hold any man in poverty by thinking he has no way of getting his good from God. Instead, I think of him as always able to tap that great spiritual Supply that God has provided for him. I know that no person, place, or thing can cheat him out of his good. Also, I know that all that is mine comes to me now perfectly under an exact and Divine law."

9. PROSPERITY AND DESIRE

"ASK AND IT SHALL BE GIVEN YOU: SEEK AND YE SHALL FIND; KNOCK AND IT SHALL BE OPENED UNTO YOU."

In any field of endeavor, there are four qualities that make for success: desire, persistence, insistence, and imagination.

Why do some men find fortunes just as easily as other men find a dime on the sidewalk? It is because they THINK BIG, ARE BIG, and ACT BIG. The law not only acts in them, but it acts in terms of multiple achievement.

How do you account for the remarkable success of George Washington Carver? DESIRE. Born of slave parents and brought up in the most abject poverty, he became one of America's most successful and prosperous men. This lowly negro not only produced four hundred twenty by-products of the peanut and sweet potato but made fortunes for those who handled them.

How do you account for the phenomenal achievements and triumphant life of Helen Keller? DESIRE, IMAGINATION, PASSION, and RESOLUTION. Born blind and deaf and dumb, she became one of America's most outstanding women. There is, too, my friend, Robert Le Tourneau, the king of earthmoving machinery. At the age of twenty-nine, he was a total failure and knew not where to turn.

Before he was middle-aged, he owned five of the largest bulldozer plants in the world. If you were to ask him the secrets of his success, he would probably give them to you in this order: a religion to live by, acceptance of stewardship, and a dynamic desire to accomplish his purpose. He not only makes fortunes for himself but gives fortunes away to others. He is the man who said, "Whatever happens, you asked for it."

Do you see what we are trying to bring out? We are thinking about you and YOUR desires; we are thinking about that job you are trying to demonstrate; we are thinking about that deal you are trying to put over. How big is your desire? How large is your vision of achievement? How deep is your feeling? Let me ask another question: Do you really have a burning passion to be the thing you want to be, to do the thing you want to do, or are you confusing wishing with desire? There is a vast difference between them. Until you get the vibration (feeling), nothing is going to happen, nothing is going to change. It is not what you say with your lips that counts but what you feel. It is God's intention that you should have an abundance of everything. Then why do you miss it? Because you water-down your desire. Because you dilute your feelings.

INSISTENCE and PERSISTENCE are equally important. We are so easily sidetracked. We allow others to change our minds and divert us from our goals. When life puts us to the test, we become discouraged, apathetic, casual and divided. Do you know what you want? Then stay with it, stick to it, persist in it, allow nothing to dissuade you. Lift your eyes to Heaven, speak squarely into that Universal Bounty, and say, "I accept that which is mine. It is here now. I feel it."

The last quality necessary to success is IMAGINATION. God's work is done. That trip you want to take – the money for the mortgage – that home – that car – they are all here. They exist in the subjective, in the invisible. Then how will you draw them into your experience? By creatively imagining them. Go into the Silence, and imagine what you want. See yourself in that new home. See yourself driving that new car. See yourself in that new job. Feel the desk before you. See your associates around you. Hold the picture in your imagination until it becomes alive and creative. Hold it until it enters your Consciousness. Believe you have the object of your desire, and thank God for it. Cultivate these four qualities, and there is nothing that you cannot get from life.

"LORD, I BELIEVE. HELP THOU MINE UNBELIEF."

10. PROSPERITY AND DISCOURAGEMENT

"HOPE THOU IN GOD."

"I am the great paralyzer of health and success. I am the great destroyer of ambition, aspiration, hope, and opportunity. I am the cause of more failure, disappointment, and wretchedness than any other one thing. I have blighted more lives, killed more initiative, ruined more plans, arrested more development, adulterated more minds, frustrated more purposes, stifled more ability, choked more talent, broken more hearts than anything else ever has. I have weakened more bodies, destroyed more health, sent more people to hospitals and insane asylums than anyone will ever know. I generate poison in the body and brain that saps life, wastes energy, cripples genius, lowers resistance, and ruins careers. I steal confidence, happiness, and peace of mind; I erect barriers and obstacles to man's good. I deprive men of money, prosperity, and opulence; I keep them in a constant state of want. I distort, distress, devitalize, demagnetize everything in human life. I starve, stunt, throttle, and thwart human effort; I keep millions of people in mediocrity and ignorance. I am the great hobgoblin of the race. I always attack people when they are down. I deceive, lie, and cheat, and yet I have more power in human life than any other one thing. The devil loves me because I am his best tool. I AM DISCOURAGEMENT."

There is but one thing that can be done for the

discouraged person and that is to show him how to re-orient his thoughts. For every effect, there is a cause. The cause of discouragement is self-centeredness, or what a psychologist calls egocentricity. The discouraged man is rich in the power to be miserable. Bounded on four sides by himself, he has shut himself off from life. He has no God but himself. Jesus said, "Whosoever will save his life shall lose it." He loses it because self-centeredness destroys itself. Consider what this means in the light of the teachings of Jesus. The center of life is God; and when man gets into the center, he presumes to take the place of God. It makes no difference what form self-centeredness may take, the harvest is always the same; the self disintegrates. When personality becomes the center of things, personality goes to pieces. Self-centeredness is its own destroyer.

How, then, shall we overcome discouragement? By crowding it out, and by giving ourselves to something bigger than ourselves. The law says that the lesser self must die in order that the greater self may live. What does that mean? It means that two lives cannot occupy the same personality at the same time any more than two thoughts can occupy the same mind at the same time. It is either one or the other. *"Ye cannot serve God and mammon."* A success thought can quickly dislodge a failure thought by a deliberate act of surrender and conscious substitution. As the courageous, constructive, and positive thoughts come in, the blue, despondent, and melancholy thoughts are crowded out.

> *"WHY ART THOU CAST DOWN, O MY SOUL? AND WHY ART THOU DISQUIETED WITHIN ME? HOPE THOU IN GOD."*

11. Prosperity and Employment

"IF THEY [THE RIGHTEOUS] *OBEY AND SERVE HIM, THEY SHALL SPEND THEIR DAYS IN PROSPERITY."*

So you are out of a job. You have looked everywhere and cannot find one. You have met disappointment after disappointment. You have been ignored, rejected, rebuffed, and turned down until you are disheartened, morbid, and scared. You are in debt and do not know how to get out of it. You are engaged and want to get married. You are married and have a family to support. You have a rapidly dwindling savings account. You will soon be in want. The very thought of it makes you frantic. Ah! There is the fly in the ointment. You are looking to that little savings account instead of to God. You are putting your faith in the wrong thing. Hasn't it occurred to you that God might do something to help you in this situation? Can *God and Company* fail? Isn't everything included in this *Company* – jobs, money, promotions, and everything else? Then, why don't you claim what you need? Why don't you accept what is rightfully yours?

"GOD IS MY EMPLOYER. I TRUST HIM TO GIVE ME MY RIGHT WORK AND TO PAY ME GENEROUSLY."

WORKING FOR RIGHT EMPLOYMENT

In working for employment or right placement, the first thing to do is to realize that you have no employer but God. Then you must realize that there is a place for you, one right place. Know that you will find it through the employment office in your own mind. GOD IS MY ONLY SUPPORT AND EMPLOYER: say these words over and over until they form in you a consciousness of the Truth they express. Don't outline or ask for a particular position, but let God guide you into that which is for your highest good. He may have something better for you than you can possibly conceive for yourself.

The next step is to realize that there is only One Activity – God-Activity – and that this Activity is expressing through you now. It knows no seasons of employment or unemployment, no hard times or good times, for it is continuous. Now hold this thought for a moment: Since God's Activity is unceasing and you are one with it, you can never be out of work. You are working for God and not man; it is God who gives you your right salary.

There is always a temptation when one is out of work to take the first job that comes along. This is often a mistake. People who get jobs by the hit-or-miss method are seldom satisfied. The right way is to find out what you are best fitted for and to work spiritually toward your right placement. If you have a plan for your life, you will reach a desirable destination. If you do not have a plan, you are likely to end up in the dog house.

Your third step should be an analysis of your abilities and potentialities. Through a vocational analysis or through self-discovery, you should determine what work you are best fitted to do. Do you like to work with tools? Do you prefer art, music, or chemistry? Are you creative? Do you like to use your hands? Do you like to teach? Make a careful analysis of yourself, seek Divine Guidance, and you cannot fail.

The fourth step is to treat yourself for the fulfillment of your desire. Use some such statement as the Mind Model that follows:

> *"I KNOW THAT THE DIVINE INTELLIGENCE WITHIN ME KNOWS WHAT MY PARTICULAR WORK IS. IT KNOWS THE RIGHT ACTIVITY TO BRING ABOUT MY OBJECTIVE. I RELY ON IT TO OPEN THE WAY AND TO SHOW ME THE SIGN THAT POINTS OUT THE RIGHT ACTION. I REALIZE THIS DIVINE GUIDANCE IS WITHIN ME NOW, AND THAT GOD-ACTIVITY CANNOT BE WITHHELD FROM MY AFFAIRS."*

The last step is to get the feeling of the fulfillment of your desire. You want a good job. Then get the feeling of it. Use your imagination. See yourself in it. Feel the desk, typewriter, or merchandise before you. Feel the tools of your trade. See your employer smiling at you and approving of what you do. Know that you are capable of meeting any demand that can be made upon you. Thank God that your desire is already fulfilled, and await its manifestation in peace and confidence.

"I CAN DO ALL THINGS THROUGH CHRIST WHICH STRENGTHENETH ME."

12. PROSPERITY AND FAULTFINDING

"WHY BEHOLDEST THOU THE MOTE THAT IS IN THY BROTHER'S EYE, BUT CONSIDEREST NOT THE BEAM THAT IS IN THINE OWN EYE?"

Here is a problem that compels our immediate attention. Read between the lines of this text, and you will see that what Jesus is really denouncing is criticism. There is a bit of humor in the text, too. Here is a man with a veritable telephone pole in his own eye who is looking for a speck in the eye of another. The point Jesus is bringing out is that the habitual critic is so busy looking for the faults and shortcomings of others that he has become blind to his own.

From our own experience, we know this is true and we also know that as the critic magnifies the faults of others, he minimizes his own. Psychiatrists tell us, too, that if he did not have these same faults or a capacity for them within himself, he could not recognize them in others.

There is another lesson here which must not be overlooked. The critical person not only has more physical troubles than the non-critical person but more financial troubles as well. He is the one who is always striving to make both ends meet; always staggering his obligations; always borrowing; always juggling; and always short. If you do not believe this, call the roll of the thousands of faultfinders who have literally criticized themselves into poverty by their ridicule and censure of others. "Like attracts like." A critical consciousness cannot demonstrate prosperity any more than a failure consciousness can demonstrate success. It is contrary to law.

"What thou seest, that thou beest." Critical thoughts are poverty thoughts directed toward others; what we habitually see in others comes to dwell with us. Thus the person who is always looking for the worst in others (seeing lack) is shortchanging himself. He is unconsciously asking that his supply be shut off. Why? God's Abundance will not flow toward a critical and censorious mind. Let us be frank with ourselves in this matter then. If we are guilty of this vicious habit, we have no one to blame for our impoverished conditions but ourselves. The fault finder throws away the good and keeps the bad. He is so busy seeing lack in others that he creates a greater lack within himself.

How then shall we overcome this wicked and futile habit? There are five practices that we must adopt:

1. Recognize that criticism always defeats its own purpose. It is destructive and disruptive and separates us from our good. It alienates us from our friends and keeps us in a state of need.

2. Make the mind a graveyard for the faults of others; never repeat any gossip.

3. Look for the best in every person, and broadcast what you find.

4. Meet every critical thought with an affirmation of truth.
5. Practice the Presence of God; the closer we keep in touch with Him the less negation we will see.

"THOU ART OF PURER EYES THAN TO BEHOLD EVIL, AND CANST NOT LOOK UPON INIQUITY."

"FORGIVE US OUR TRESPASSES AS WE FORGIVE THOSE WHO TRESPASS AGAINST US."

13. PROSPERITY AND FEAR

"PERFECT LOVE CASTETH OUT FEAR."

What word brings more disaster, poverty, tragedy, and misfortune into human life than any other? What word condemns more men to failure, penury, and want than any other? What is the word that retards man's progress and places obstructions in his path? What word causes more worry, lack of confidence, timidity, anxiety, self-depreciation, irresolution, balefulness, and depression than any other? What is the word that lays the foundation for more disease, sickness, and misery than any other? What word destroys confidence, hope, happiness, joy, and peace of mind? What word never adds anything to your health, wealth, comfort, or happiness? What word wastes your mental powers, saps your energy, destroys your efficiency, paralyzes your effort, and cuts down your chances of success? What word cramps your mind, stifles your life, and limits your powers of expressing? What word destroys ambition, weakens character, shakes confidence, and keeps millions in mediocrity?

Have you guessed it? The word is *fear.* Fear is the foundation of all our financial difficulties because it reverses the Law of Attraction. Fear is faith turned upside down. It is faith in evil. When we fear want or failure, we attract it to ourselves just as surely as though we desired it. That is why Job said, *"The thing I greatly feared has come upon me and that which I was afraid of is come unto me."* By fearing evil, he gave it the power to operate in his life.

The Law of Fear works in two ways just as all other laws do. It either draws the thing you fear toward you, or it forces you toward it. That is why the object of fear is likened to a moth fluttering around a flame. If you do not change your position in the Law (reverse the thought), you will be consumed by it. Why is this true? Because whatever you give your attention to absorbs you. If you give fear the best seat in your mental household, you will attract as guests not only poverty, penury, and want but all the mental vampires that are the progeny of fear.

"God hath not given us the spirit of fear; but of power, and of love, and of a sound mind." According to the law of heredity, man is entitled to but two fears – the fear of falling and the fear of loud noises.

Where did the other eight or nine thousand fears come from? They were man-made. They came out of negative religion and maladjustment to life. How can we unmake them? We have the answer in two words – *repentance* and *salvation.* The word *repent* means turning around and the word *salvation* means a safe return. Those two words should mean to you: Change your mind (reverse the thought), and get back to God. Nothing difficult about that. Just fill your mind with thoughts of courage, confidence, faith, and assurance, and your fears will disappear.

"YEA, THOUGH I WALK THROUGH THE VALLEY OF THE SHADOW OF DEATH, I WILL FEAR NO EVIL: FOR THOU ART WITH ME; THY ROD AND THY STAFF, THEY COMFORT ME...SURELY GOODNESS AND MERCY SHALL FOLLOW ME ALL THE DAYS OF MY LIFE."

14. PROSPERITY AND FINANCIAL REVERSES

"MY SOUL, WAIT THOU ONLY UPON GOD: FOR MY
EXPECTATION IS FROM HIM."

People always have a tendency to become panicky and fearful when they meet with financial reverses. In the vernacular of the street, they become *tight.* They develop an attitude that contracts their income instead of expanding it. Some will even go so far as to curtail or to cancel their giving to the support of God's work. It is not contraction we need at such a time but expansion. Pinching one's savings complicates the problem rather than simplifies it. Adversity is not the time to give less but more. The words, *miser* and *miserable,* come from the same root.

The solution to financial difficulties is not to break the contact between supply and demand but to strengthen it. Giving and spending not only preserve and strengthen this contact but keep our affairs in touch with Creative Power. You recall that *"the younger son"* voluntarily separated himself and his inheritance from his father and that this separation led to the wasting of his substance and his encounter with famine. If we practice stringent economy in times like these, if we entertain doubt, fear, and worry, if we deprive ourselves of the comforts of life, if we indulge in thoughts of failure and defeat, if we buy cheap clothes, cheap food, if we spend all our time watching little things, if we put a nickel in the contribution box and think too much about our losses, we separate ourselves from God's good. What we need at such a time is not cowardice and parsimony but courage and liberality.

"The destruction of the poor," says the Bible, *"is their poverty."* That is, their poverty-stricken attitude keeps away their prosperity. Dr. Perry Green believes that "Job's lament – *'The thing which I greatly feared is come upon* me' – should be changed to read, 'The thing which I was greatly conscious of has come upon me.'" In other words, it is the inner thought and feeling that take tangible form in our lives.

"As a man thinketh in his heart [in his consciousness], *so is he* [outwardly]." If he pinches in his mind (cuts his standard of giving and living and refuses to pay his bills), he pinches the flow of his supply. A penury consciousness not only tightens the purse strings so that nothing can get out, but it is equally successful in keeping anything from getting in.

The first step in getting out of financial difficulties is to get rid of all thoughts of lack, poverty, and insufficiency. Can't God take just as good care of you during a depression as He can during a boom?

The second step is to establish the conviction that all that the Father has is yours. Your supply is not coming to you; it is already here. It cannot be kept from you; it cannot be delayed. If you specialize the Law for your good, nothing of an evil or negative character can act upon you or be a law unto you.

The third step is to realize that your situation is not so bad as it seems. You have never starved before and you are not going to starve now.

The fourth step is to keep your standards high. Do not cripple your mind and feelings with small and foolish economies.

The fifth step is to use what you have and to trust God for the increase.

"THERE IS NO FEAR IN LOVE; BUT PERFECT LOVE CASTETH OUT FEAR: BECAUSE FEAR HATH TORMENT."

15. PROSPERITY AND FORGIVENESS

"GO IN PEACE, AND BE WHOLE OF THY PLAGUE."

Forgiving your debtors is like preventive medicine. The act of forgiving keeps you from falling into debt yourself. Did Jesus mean that you were to cancel the obligations of those who owe you money and mark their accounts paid? Not at all. It is not the debt that Jesus expects you to cancel (forgive) but the burdensome thought and idea of debt.

The spiritual way of collecting money that is owed to you is not by sending receipted bills to those who are indebted to you but by sending them a forgiving thought. Go over your accounts carefully each day; call each debtor by name and treat him for prosperity. Tell him that you forgive the idea of debt or lack that you have been holding against him. Do it sincerely and purposefully, and you will be surprised at the way the money will come in.

The reason Jesus laid so much emphasis upon forgiveness between creditor and debtor was to break the bondage that grows up between them. When the payment of a debt is long overdue, there are bound to be hard, critical, condemnatory, and uncharitable thoughts. These not only increase the debtor's lack and drive him farther away but they make it harder for him to pay. The better way is to pray for the debtor, to bless him with thoughts of abundance. Many people think of forgiving an enemy as conferring a favor upon him. In a sense this is true, but the one who forgives is the real beneficiary. To forgive is not only to forget. or to overlook, but to heal.

The next thing to remember about forgiveness is that others always tend to live up to our expectations. If we expect the worst and think the worst of a person. we attract the worst from him. If we think the best and speak the best of those who are indebted to us, we attract their best. It is greatly to our advantage to cultivate an attitude of love and well-being toward our debtors. Instead of thinking, feeling, and saying unkind things about them, let us fill our minds with thoughts of forgiveness, love, peace, and abundance. Let us meet every critical, doubtful, and unjust thought with the statement: *"There is now no condemnation in Christ Jesus."*

"I NOW RADIATE THE LIVING CURRENT OF MY FORGIVENESS INTO ALL THE WORLD, AND INTO THE HEARTS OF ALL MEN AND WOMEN, KNOWN AND UNKNOWN, IN THE FLESH OR IN THE SPIRIT, WHO HAVE IN ANY WAY TRESPASSED AGAINST ME, THAT THEY MAY BE FOREVER SEPARATED AND SET FREE FROM THEIR SIN.

"I KNOW THAT THIS SAME CURRENT OF FORGIVING POWER WILL RETURN, BEARING TO ME THE FULL FORGIVENESS OF MY GOD FOR MY TRESPASSES AGAINST HIM."

16. PROSPERITY AND GIVING

"ALL THINGS COME OF THEE, AND OF THINE OWN
HAVE WE GIVEN THEE."

Perhaps the greatest stumbling block to those seeking to demonstrate prosperity is the Law of Giving and Receiving. They can see no connection between stewardship and abundance, between giving and getting, in spite of the clear command of Jesus: *"Give and it shall be given unto you."* They can see no reason why giving should precede receiving or why the spirit in which they give should govern the amount that they receive.

Daniel Webster once said, "The most solemn thought I have ever had – and I have it often – is my personal accountability to Almighty God." It is a solemn thought that some day you and I must give an account to Almighty God for the money and goods that He has lent to us. Why do we say "lent to us"? Because everything belongs to God. Then why must we give generously in order to receive abundantly? There are eight reasons:

1. To keep a reciprocal action between God's Supply and our purse, between the relative and the Absolute (earth and Heaven).

2. To keep the mind relaxed and free of cramped, limited, narrow, parsimonious, pinched, strained, and warped thoughts.

3. To keep the attention centered in God and independent of things.

4. To demonstrate to the world that our security depends upon God and not on money. To confuse money *per se* with prosperity shuts off our supply and destroys our prosperity. Stagnation sets in; where there is stagnation, there is disintegration.

5. To prove that we accept our stewardship as the acid test of our faith in Universal Supply.

6. To stimulate the growth and expansion of Consciousness, and to quicken the Law of Attraction.

7. To harness our desires to what we want by releasing what we have. If there is a strangle hold on what we have, it cannot circulate and attract its friends. The law says that what we desire and expect is what we create.

8. To maintain a balance in mind and body that results in happiness, health, and wellbeing.

"KEEP THEREFORE THE WORDS OF THIS COVENANT, AND DO THEM, THAT YE MAY PROSPER IN ALL THAT YE DO."

17. PROSPERITY AND GIVING CHEERFULLY

"HE WHICH SOWETH SPARINGLY SHALL REAP ALSO SPARINGLY: AND HE WHICH SOWETH BOUNTIFULLY SHALL REAP ALSO BOUNTIFULLY. EVERY MAN ACCORDING AS HE PURPOSETH IN HIS HEART, SO LET HIM GIVE; NOT GRUDGINGLY, OR OF NECESSITY: FOR GOD LOVETH A CHEERFUL GIVER."

Why are we asked to give bountifully to spiritual enterprises? Because such giving opens our faculties to receive. Bountiful giving is the gift and the giver in one parcel. God looks not upon the monetary value of the gift but upon the spirit of the giver. Our gifts are not measured in terms of dollars and cents but in terms of what we have. The widow's mite given out of *"her want"* was more than the gifts of those who *"cast in of their abundance."*

Read the text in the Greek, and you will see that the word translated cheerful is *hilarion.* Among the synonyms for the word *hilarity,* we find glee, mirth, gayety, exhilaration. God loves an hilarious giver because he proves his absolute faith in the formless substance of God. His giving shows his confidence that as he metes it shall be measured to him again. He knows that there is always more where his present supply came from.

Someone has shown the need for movement in these

words: "What would happen if all the electricity should suddenly refuse to move on over the wires? If water stood still in the mains? If yesterday's air refused to rise and make way for today's? It would be disastrous. Well, that is exactly what man causes to happen with the money currents."

What does the law say? *"Whatsoever a man soweth that shall he also reap."* You keep only what you give away. If you would catch the big fish, launch out into deep waters. Give with abandon. Give lavishly. Give cheerfully.

The relationship that exists between our attitude and our prosperity is shown in the edict given to the Israelites: *"Because thou servedest not the Lord thy God with joyfulness, and with gladness of heart, for the abundance of all things; therefore, shalt thou serve thine enemies . . . in hunger, and in thirst, and in nakedness, and in want of all things."* It doesn't make any difference how much money or how little we may have, God requires us to let it go and to do so cheerfully. Is that hard to do? Not when we accept the promises of security and realize that sharing is the key to an abundance of the world's wealth.

"IN THE DAY OF PROSPERITY, BE JOYFUL."

18. PROSPERITY AND HUMAN THOUGHT

"TAKE NO THOUGHT FOR THE MORROW."

The injunction, *"Take no thought,"* does not refer to a thoughtless and indolent state of existence but to living without thought of anxiety and fear. It is one thing to plan for the future, and another thing to worry about it. *"Take therefore no thought for the morrow: for the morrow shall take thought of the things of itself. Sufficient unto the day is the evil thereof."* This idea was new to the people who heard it, and they were no doubt puzzled by it. How could a man make a living without looking ahead? How could he accomplish anything without taking thought? Listen to the challenge of Jesus: *"Which of you by taking thought can add one cubit unto his stature?"* Do you get the meaning in that question? It is just as though He had asked, "What can you accomplish by worry?" Jesus did not mean that a man was to sit around and do nothing. He did not mean that he was to pass all his problems and responsibilities to God. Work is one of the greatest blessings in the world; if you do not believe that it is, ask the man in solitary confinement. Everyone must do some kind of useful work; to work with enthusiasm and happiness, with freedom from fear and worry, is to *"take no thought."*

But there is another lesson here. There is a warning against the fictitious and shallow thinking of the human mind;

in other words, thinking without spirit, thinking without manifestation. The Bible refers to this kind of thinking as *"clouds without rain,"* and the metaphysician speaks of it as prayer without answer. There are, briefly, two kinds of thinking: right thinking which is due to the action of the Holy Spirit, and wrong thinking which is due to the action of the carnal or human mind. One process is thinking through God (or allowing God to think through us); the other is thinking through the self, or through matter. The thought that Jesus referred to is the latter. It is thinking around *(of* and *about)* things with all the limitations that reversed (upside down) thinking implies. It is the kind of thought-taking that has its foundation in the wisdom of man which, as the Bible says, *"is foolishness with God."* Can you by the thought process alone fathom the mystery of feeding five thousand people with five loaves of bread and two small fishes? The human mind has no comprehension of the power of Substance to increase and multiply itself.

"Therefore take no thought, saying, What shall we eat? or, What shall we drink? or, Wherewithal shall we be clothed? ... for your heavenly Father knoweth that ye have need of all these things. But seek ye first the Kingdom of God [seek to let God think through you] *... and all these things shall be added unto you."*

HE *"PREPAREST A TABLE BEFORE ME."*

19. Prosperity and Imagination

"DANIEL HAD UNDERSTANDING IN ALL VISIONS AND DREAMS."

Webster says *imagination* is "that power or function of the mind whereby we have ideal experience; primarily, the power or process of having mental images: broadly, the power or process of forming ideal constructions from images, concepts and feelings, with relative freedom from objective restraint...a conception or imaging of some event; a scheme, a plot or project... expectation." The Latin word for image is *imago;* it comes from the same root as the word that means to imitate.

The Book of Proverbs tells us, *"Where there is no vision* [imagination], *the people perish."*

Napoleon said, "Imagination rules the world."

Bernard Shaw says through the lips of Cauchon in his play, "Saint Joan": "Is it not a pity that a Christ must die in torment in every age to save those who have no imagination?"

Imagination is not only the basic factor in all creative achievement, progress, and invention, but it is also the basic factor in all healing, health, demonstration, success, and supply. Our bodies, like our purses, are quickly affected by our imagination. Many have imagined themselves into certain diseases; and many by reversing the process have imagined themselves out of them. If we see ourselves in sickness, poverty, and failure, we shall produce these conditions; if we image ourselves in health, wealth, and success, we shall produce these. The result is a matter of imagination. We build or destroy, heal or suffer, prosper or want, fail or succeed according to the use we make of the imaging faculty of the mind.

Actually there are no imperfect demonstrations of the power of mind on the material plane. Every circumstance and condition in our lives is the fulfillment of the promise: *"All things whatsoever ye shall ask in prayer* [imagination – because we must image what we pray for] *believing, ye shall receive."*

Charles Fillmore says, "Someone started the idea of lack and we tuned in: we kept tuning in and accepting the thought, until we finally convinced ourselves that it was true. Spiritual substance obeyed this command or belief and filled the order for us. The channels through which the order was delivered do not alter the fact that the filling was the result of creative intelligence made evident by a very natural process – *the imagination.*

To imagine a thing is to make a mold with our thoughts. That is our part. God's part is to pour the Substance into the mold. This Substance is all about us, waiting to form itself around our thoughts and to bring into our lives the things about which we are thinking. If we wish prosperity, we must keep our minds off scarcity and on plenty. If we imagine that we are opulent and successful in everything we do, our thoughts will act on this formless Substance with that idea. If we think abundance and plenty all the time, abundance has to express itself in all our affairs.

> *"A GOOD MAN OUT OF THE GOOD TREASURE OF HIS HEART BRINGETH FORTH THAT WHICH IS GOOD."*

20. PROSPERITY AND JUST RETURN
(Law of Non-Possession)

"THE EARTH IS THE LORD'S AND THE FULLNESS
THEREOF."

When we understand that all the money belongs to God and that we are only stewards over it, we shall see that proportionate giving is not only the true basis of prosperity but the secret of continuous and uninterrupted supply. Giving is the guarantee of true and abundant prosperity. Everybody wants a larger income, but a larger income depends upon a more accurate use and application of Divine Law. Jesus stated the Law to the disciples: *"Give, and it shall be given unto you; good measure, pressed down, and shaken together, and running over, shall men give into your bosom. For with the same measure that ye mete withal it shall be measured to you again."* Do you catch the import of that? Before you can get fresh water from your faucet, the old water must flow out. If you wish a full flow of water, you must turn the faucet on full force. So it is with money. If you cut off or narrow down the stream that flows out to others, you interfere with the supply that is waiting to flow in.

St. Paul said, *"On the first day of the week let each of you lay by him in store, as God hath prospered him."* You should think of your stewardship not as giving to man, church, or a specific relief fund but to God. Your pledge is a covenant between Him and you. Neither should you think of your supply as corning from clients, customers, or employers; you should recognize it as corning from God. In giving to Him and His work, you are simply preserving the contact between your supply and your demand; you are supporting and perpetuating your income. If there is a break in this process, your income must diminish accordingly.

The first step in building a spirit of generosity is to practice the Law of Non-Possession. All the money in the universe belongs to God; we as individuals possess nothing. Must we then give up all our material possessions? Not at all. We are not to give up our possessions, but to release anxiety, worry, fear, and tension that attaches to them. *"Go, sell all that thou hast."* When the sense of possession and sense of responsibility go, the fear (which is the cause of our poverty) will go, too.

The second step is to think of ourselves as stewards, or distributors of God's gifts. As stewards, we not only open ourselves to greater income, but we set in motion a law that balances the elements in our lives. Without balance, there is decay, disintegration, disease, and lack. With balance, there is plenty for every need. *"They that seek the Lord shall not want any good thing."* When we lift our Consciousness to Christ's standard of giving, we shall lift our income to the level of our wants.

The third step is to remember that there is no charity,

that there are no benefactors, no dependents, and no paupers. If all the money belongs to God and we are all His children, everyone has the same right to it that we have. The fact that we give to religious and community organizations means merely that we are exercising our stewardship toward them. We give not to another's poverty but to his prosperity.

The fourth step is to know that in sharing we are giving ourselves. We are giving our energy, our labor, our time, our wisdom, and our skill minted into currency, dollars, and cents. We are releasing life.

"THE GIFT WITHOUT THE GIVER IS BARE."

21. PROSPERITY AND THE KINGDOM

(Investments)

"LAY NOT UP FOR YOURSELVES TREASURES UPON EARTH, WHERE MOTH AND RUST DOTH CORRUPT, AND WHERE THIEVES BREAK THROUGH AND STEAL: BUT LAY UP FOR YOURSELVES TREASURES IN HEAVEN, WHERE NEITHER MOTH NOR RUST DOTH CORRUPT, AND WHERE THIEVES DO NOT BREAK THROUGH AND STEAL."

The injunction, "Do not put all your eggs in one basket," means that your reserves should not all be put in one place. "Scatter them," says the wise banker, "so that your losses may be compensated by gains. If you invest everything in one enterprise, you may lose all you have." Astute business men get the advice of experts before investing their money, for they want safety as well as dividends. However, when a depression comes, we realize how little any man knows about the real laws of wealth. But there is One within us who does know. There is One who will not only show us how to get the largest possible dividends from our investments but who will see that we have everything needful to our good.

Jesus is giving us the advice of an expert. He is telling us where to invest our capital for the greatest returns. He is giving us the understanding of the One who ordained the Law in the first place. It makes no difference how much capital a man may have, there are but two places in which he may invest it. He can either lay it up upon the earth, or he can lay it up in Heaven. There is no second, third, or fourth place in which he may invest. Everybody has capital of some kind. Everybody is investing it in one of these two places.

It is important, therefore, that we understand this advice of Jesus and know why He directs us to one place instead of another. Since our choice is limited to one of two places, we must know why one is better than the other. If a friend advised us to go to one investment house instead of another or to purchase one stock instead of another, we should want to know the reasons for his choice.

We think we want information about stocks, bonds, and mortgages; we believe that we are looking for gilt-edged securities that will stand up in any kind of a crisis; and we are. But underneath all this seeking is the search for God. We may call it prosperity, we may call it security, we may call it health, we may call it happiness, but in the final analysis, it is that which is permanent, enduring, and true. We want treasures in Heaven.

What does it mean to lay up treasures upon earth? It means to put money and the things it represents first in our thoughts and affections. By putting money above its Source (loving the symbol rather than the spirit that it expresses), man limits it. *"It is easier for a camel to go through the eye of a needle than for a rich man to enter the Kingdom of God."* If your life purpose is to acquire riches, it is proof that you love money rather than the Substance that lies back of it.

To lay up treasures in Heaven is to lay up rich ideas in mind. But what good are rich ideas when one is financially flat on his back? Rich ideas can be translated into currency, houses, positions, automobiles, or anything else that we need, according to our thought. When we understand that all riches are spiritual and within the reach of all as divine ideas, we shall understand why Jesus told us to lay up treasures in Mind. Spiritual investments will meet our needs now and will satisfy our needs in the life to come.

"...AN INHERITANCE INCORRUPTIBLE AND UNDEFILED,...THAT FADETH NOT AWAY."

22. PROSPERITY AND THE LAW

"THE LAW OF THE LORD IS PERFECT."

The law governing the manifestation of supply is just as exact and unerring as the laws of electricity, gravitation, or mathematics. One of the first things we learned in our study of metaphysics was a definition of law. Do you remember it? *Law is Mind in action.* God's Life, Substance, and Power act through the Law. We are surrounded by a formless, omnipresent, thinking Substance – infinite, impersonal, subjective, neutral, plastic. All things are made from this one Universal Substance and are permeated, penetrated, and interpenetrated by It. As man individualizes this Law, he creates by his word.

We hear a great deal in metaphysical circles bout demonstration, but the word has been greatly misunderstood. What we really mean by demonstration is the automatic outworking of the Law that *"As a man thinketh in his heart, so is he."* What do these words mean? They mean that thoughts held in the mind ultimately take form in the outer world. Jesus was very clear about this action: *"Whatsoever a man soweth, that shall he also reap."* Evil thoughts manifest evil just as quickly as good thoughts manifest good. We must keep our thoughts constructive, positive, and life-giving if we desire happiness, prosperity, and life.

The next step is to apply the Law, or to speak our word

into it. How are we told to do this? *"Ask – believing."* The only obligation or responsibility we ever have is to accept and believe. Where does the Law come in? It doesn't come in; it is already in. We are simply completing a circuit. Since the Kingdom of God is within man, as Jesus said, and since God is All-Good, every good thing that man can possibly desire is already within him, waiting to come forth. It is there as an idea that becomes flesh (materializes) through the prayer of acceptance; that is, through asking and believing. First, we make our claim through an affirmation that completely embodies our desire. This is a push button, so to speak, that connects our consciousness with God's Consciousness and sets the Law in motion. Then we pray the prayer of faith, or completely accept the idea embodied in the claim. Then, as Ernest Holmes says, "The law operates upon our acceptance through our belief, at the level of our faith, according to our recognition." *"As thou hast believed,* so *be it done unto thee."*

Let us suppose that you desire to increase your income to meet special needs. Your first step is to affirm: "God's wealth is quickened in me, and my needs are abundantly supplied." Speak your word with firmness and deep conviction. The next step is the prayer of acceptance.

"LET THIS TRUTH BE QUICKENED (MADE ACTIVE AND ALIVE) IN ME AS A REVELATION TO MY CONSCIOUS MIND OF GOD'S IMMEDIATE

RESPONSE TO MY NEEDS. THERE IS NOTHING IN ME THAT CONTRADICTS, DENIES, OR NEUTRALIZES MY WORD. MY WHOLE MIND ACCEPTS THE FULFILLMENT OF THIS DESIRE. MY WHOLE BEING RESPONDS TO IT. I THANK THEE, FATHER, THAT I AM ABLE TO APPROPRIATE THY WEALTH AND MEET ALL MY NEEDS."

23. PROSPERITY AND THE MAGNET

(Law of Attraction)

"I FILL MY MIND SO FULL OF THOUGHTS OF PROSPERITY THAT THERE IS NO ROOM FOR A THOUGHT OF WANT."

This Mind Model deals with the Law of Attraction and Expulsion. It gets rid of thoughts of poverty and want by substituting thoughts of opulence and plenty. How is this change accomplished? It is done by withdrawing the thought from lack and insufficiency and dwelling upon the all-providing Substance of God. We crowd out the limited and impoverished thought by filling every corner of the mind full of rich and prosperous thoughts.

Like attracts like, fear attracts fear, failure attracts failure, and poverty attracts poverty. Criticism attracts more criticism, bitterness attracts more bitterness, and loss attracts more loss. Every impression tends to become an expression. This is the Law of Attraction. What you hold in the mind, what you think about, visualize, and dwell upon will not only build itself into your life but will increase your power of attraction for that thing. Prosperity is just a matter of obeying the Law of Attraction. The Law will always bring to you the things and conditions that are like the thoughts and convictions that dominate your mind. If you are attracting the wrong things, you can change the action of the Law by changing the kind of attraction you have. You can do it by determining what sort of a magnet, your mind will be. The Law of Increase is just as exact as the law of mathematics. It operates just as unerringly. Wealth like poverty starts in the mind; one is just as much a demonstration as the other. Either one must be thought of before it becomes a reality. There is no evading this Law. If you would attract prosperity, you must not only keep your mind saturated with prosperous ideas, you must also keep it free from poverty ideas.

> *"THIS ONE THING I DO, FORGETTING THOSE THINGS WHICH ARE BEHIND, AND REACHING FORTH UNTO THOSE THINGS WHICH ARE BEFORE, I PRESS TOWARD THE MARK."*

24. PROSPERITY AND NEGATIVE THOUGHT

"I CONSCIOUSLY CLEAR THE CHANNELS OF MY THOUGHT, FEELING, AND ACTION SO THAT PROSPERITY MAY FLOW FREELY THROUGH ME."

To demonstrate prosperity one must provide a free, clear, and open channel for its reception. It will not flow through channels choked by parsimony, fear, worry, despair, discouragement, or doubt. A generous attitude, broad vision, and wide outlook are the best assurance of success. Ask yourself why it is that the penny-pincher never does big things, and your answer will be that his close, limited, mean, stingy, narrow attitude shuts off his supply. He cannot do big things because his mind is forever occupied with little things. Try to explain why a generous spirit is the sanest economy, and you must recognize that generosity gauges the flow of supply. When we try to possess things, we are affected just as we are as when we try to hold our breath. The act of holding causes congestion and pain, a result we call stagnation. When the circulation of the blood is restricted at any point in the body, there is pain at that point; any hindrance to the flow of God's Substance results in deprivation of some kind to someone. Cramped, mean, parsimonious, warped thoughts diminish one's supply, but abundant, big, broad, generous, and joyous thoughts increase it. It is not a man's natural ability that determines his prosperity and success but his Consciousness of Abundance.

How is a poverty concept to be overcome? By affirming prosperity until the negative thought is neutralized.

Why do some people fail to demonstrate prosperity? There are three reasons:

1. They have a belief in separation from God.
2. They fail to provide a mental equivalent of greater good.
3. They lack gratitude for what they already have.

What are the things that must be neutralized before prosperity can come in? Fear, worry, resentment, envy, jealousy, gossip, criticism, and the race belief in poverty. The business man must not only reject the fear of competition and limitation, but the belief in peak and depression. When the Consciousness of Prosperity is firmly established in one, it will produce prosperity whether there is a presidential election or not. Politics and depression have no power against a Consciousness of Plenty.

TREATMENT FOR PROSPERITY

"I, John Smith, am a center in Divine Mind, a point of God-Conscious Life, Truth, and Action. I am God's son with God's attributes. My affairs are Divinely guarded and guided into right action, into correct results. Everything I think, say, or do is stimulated by the Truth. There is power in my word because it is the Truth. There is continuous right action in my life and affairs. All belief in wrong action is dispelled. Right action alone has Power and is Power; and Power is God, the Living Spirit Almighty.

"This Spirit animates everything that I think, say, and do. Divine ideas come to me daily. They direct and sustain me continuously. I do the right thing at the right time, say the right word at the right time, and follow the right course at the right time.

"All suggestions of age, poverty, limitation or unhappiness are uprooted from my thought. I am happy, well, and filled with perfect life. I live in the spirit of Truth and am conscious that it abides in me. My word is the law unto its own manifestation; it brings fulfillment. There is no unbelief, doubt, nor uncertainty. All doubt vanishes from my mind; the truth makes me free. I release this word to Creative Mind, with faith and gratitude, knowing it will be done unto me as I believe. And it is so." (Ernest Holmes, *The Science of Mind*)

25. PROSPERITY AND OBEDIENCE

"IF YE BE WILLING AND OBEDIENT, YE SHALL EAT THE GOOD OF THE LAND."

When electricity fails. the problem is not in the current but in the appliances through which it passes. When mathematics fails, the problem is not in the principle but in our understanding of it. When prayer fails, the problem is not in the Law but in our relationship to it.

The Law of Prosperity is a Law of Consciousness. It is a divine connection in mind which must be kept free and open through observance of the Law. If Consciousness is the cause of everything that comes into our lives, we must keep our thinking, feeling, and acting in line with wealth and not with poverty. St. James said, *"Every good and every perfect gift is from above, and cometh down from the Father of lights, with whom is no variableness, neither shadow of turning."* Note the words, *no variableness,* and compare the thought with St. Paul's *"Jesus Christ the same yesterday, and today, and for ever."*

The price we pay for prosperity is living and thinking in strict obedience and conformity to law. In order to receive from God, we must be receptive to His Good. We must cultivate receptivity by eliminating all the negative thoughts, feelings, and practices that close our channels of supply. We must pay the price of receptivity. We must pay the price of giving, and we must pay the price of receiving.

Jesus said, *"He that gathereth not with Me scattereth abroad."* We are either moving with the Law, or we are moving against it. There are no half-way measures with the Law, and there is no chance of breaking it. If we try to break it, it breaks us. It works for our good only if its conditions are fulfilled. It has no purpose but to obey its own terms. St. Paul tells us that we must bring *"into captivity every thought to the obedience of Christ."* We must keep the rules. We must do everything that is required of us. If we want good results, we must go all the way. We must turn the other cheek. We must give our cloak with our coat. We must go the second mile. We must forgive *"seventy times seven"* times. We must render *"unto Caesar the things that are Caesar's."*

Analyze these rules carefully, and you will see that your failure to demonstrate prosperity has been due to some departure from the Law. You will see that even the most trivial thoughts come back to you in tangible form. A thousandth-of-an-inch variation from specifications in the machining of an engine shaft will produce friction enough in its bearings to ruin them. Keep looking until you find the variation. It may be gossip or lying that is pinching your income. It may be faultfinding or criticism. Did you ever stop to think that when you see the faults of others you are really looking at your own negative thoughts about them? The subconscious mind accepts these thoughts as commands and sets about to bring them home to you. When we go all the way in keeping the law, we get the fulfillment of our desires.

"THEN PETER ANSWERED AND SAID, WE OUGHT TO OBEY GOD RATHER THAN MEN."

26. PROSPERITY AND PRAISE – I

"BLESS THE LORD, O MY SOUL, AND FORGET NOT ALL HIS BENEFITS."

The greatest antidote for despondent, dejected, and depressed states of mind is praise. *"Praise is comely for the upright." "Whoso offereth praise glorifieth Me." "All thy works shall praise Thee."* The unemployed person with an empty purse and no prospects is usually a morose, gloomy, and pessimistic person. He is depressed because he is taking a half view of things. He is without hope because he has separated himself from his Source. Instead of looking toward prosperity and success, he is looking toward poverty and failure. He is what the Bible refers to as a *"broken spirit,"* and *"A broken spirit drieth the bones."* He who lets his mental level down is a sick man. The pessimism of his spirit lays a withering blight on all the activities and functions of his life. He becomes a magnet, so to speak, for all that is depressing, disillusioning, and disappointing.

If such a man were to come to me for help, I would prescribe for him the medicine of praise. I would show him how praise lifts us quickly into the realm of richness, fullness, and completeness, and how it re-unites us with the never-failing Source of Supply. I would tell him the story of Paul and Silas in prison and how praise broke their shackles and opened prison doors. I would remind him of Paul's command:

"Rejoice in the Lord always: and again I say, Rejoice"; and of the consolation of Eliphaz for Job: *"When men are cast down...there is a lifting up."* Everyone needs to practice the art of praise and rejoicing, but more especially those who are desperate, depressed, dejected, and despondent. The power of praising will not only drive pain and disease from the body but gloom and depression from the mind. Praise is one of the great lubricants of life.

The habit of praise promotes youth and health and sharpens and increases the faculties of the mind. Praise is another name for God. It not only causes all things to work together for good but helps to transmute misfortune into blessings. More praise will bring more of everything good into your life. It will open up the channels of Supply and bring you into conscious Oneness with the Divine Source. It will break the belief in poverty and set you on the road to prosperity. It will expand your consciousness, overcome obstacles, increase your power, strengthen your faith; it will make you more optimistic, more cheerful, more effective, more useful, more successful. In short, it will recreate, refresh, and rejuvenate your whole life.

It is important, therefore, that you rejoice continually. Praise God for all His blessings. Praise Him for what you have and for what you hope to get. Praise Him for your life and its possibilities. Be happy. Be glad. Be joyous now. God does not want you to grow sad, sour, dry, and miserable over losses, failures, unemployment, debts, mortgages, and hard times. He wants you to prove Him. He wants you to transmute these unhappy experiences into joyous ones through praise. By praising God, you magnify the good. You multiply His goodness in your body, in your purse, and in your affairs.

"MY SOUL DOTH MAGNIFY THE LORD, AND MY SPIRIT HATH REJOICED IN GOD MY SAVIOR."

27. PROSPERITY AND PRAISE – II

*"I WILL BLESS THE LORD AT ALL TIMES: HIS PRAISE
SHALL CONTINUALLY BE IN MY MOUTH."*

Jesus understood the prayer of Thanksgiving. You recall that before there was any tangible evidence of the answer He said, *"Father, I thank Thee that Thou hast heard me. And I know that Thou hearest me always."* It was not His words alone that caused the power to come into manifestation. *"Father, I thank Thee"* is the full recognition and realization that the thing you asked for is taking place right HERE and NOW. *"He that hath the spirit* [Consciousness] *hath the sign, also."* God's riches flow to us from every source; whole-souled gratitude opens wide the mind to receive.

Is there a momentous and important decision that you must make? Do you need guidance and wisdom? Say each time the need presents itself to your mind: "Father, I thank Thee for this direction." Then see how quickly the guidance will come.

Is there a problem in your home, office, business, or personal life that you have been unable to solve? Then say each time it comes to you, "Father, I thank Thee for the solution to this problem." See how quickly the answer will come.

Are you depressed, anxious, or fearful over some situation that you do not seem able to control? Then repeat these words, "God, I thank Thee." Note how quickly your state of mind will become confident and courageous. *"In everything, give thanks."*

Are you so sick that nothing seems to do you any good? Then say every time your condition comes to mind, "Father, I thank Thee for my perfect healing." Watch how quickly you will begin to improve.

Are you in debt and need money? Then say each time the thought comes to your mind, "Father, I thank Thee for the fulfillment of my need." Then watch the money come.

Give thanks instead of complaining. Give thanks instead of fearing. Give thanks instead of worrying. Give thanks instead of wondering. *"God* is *a very present help in time of trouble."* But he cannot help you unless you accept His help on spiritual terms. You must approach Him from the standpoint of having what you ask for. You must accept His help through your attitude of praise and thanksgiving. If there is nothing in your consciousness that doubts, denies, or contradicts your word, He will supply everything in abundant measure. "There is no great and no small to the soul that maketh all," Seven dollars or seven million dollars, headache or cancer – it is all the same to God.

The promise is that *"Whatsoever ye shall ask of the Father IN MY NAME* [Consciousness], *He will give it to you."* You do not have to beg God for anything; you only have to enter His Nature [Consciousness] and you can take from the

Universe anything you need. Is there anything unusual about a potter producing pottery? About a jeweler producing jewelry? About a baker producing bread? A composer producing music? Is there anything unusual about a man in Christ Consciousness doing the works of Jesus?

"WITH THANKSGIVING, LET YOUR REQUESTS BE MADE KNOWN UNTO GOD."

28. PROSPERITY AND PROPERTY

"YOUR FATHER KNOWETH WHAT THINGS YE HAVE NEED OF."

The first thing to do in disposing of a piece of property is to resolve it into an idea. In reality, you do not possess this property. It is in your hands as a steward. It is merely an idea that you are through with and ready to pass on to someone else. Make sure, however, that you are through with it. By that I mean, make sure that you have released it in your thought, or it will keep coming back on your hands.

The author was once asked to work metaphysically for the immediate sale of a large and expensive mountain home. The results were almost instantaneous. A buyer appeared in a very few days and made a deposit of five thousand dollars. Everyone was happy about it; but the deal did not go through, and the house came back to the original owners. There was great disappointment, and assistance was called for again. The house came back a second time, and then it was found that one of the owners was still holding on. She loved the house so much that she could not part with it in her thought. When it was explained to her why she must let go, the deal was finally consummated.

In *Good Business,* we are told that "The Truth student who invokes Divine Principle to aid in the sale of lots, farms, houses, or business buildings, for himself or for another, does not work to the end that a specific piece of property may be disposed of at a specific price. He keeps his mind fixed upon the spiritual aspect of such a sale by realizing that the owner of the property is a channel through which a home or other good gift is distributed from the Creator of all good to His children. The student knows that if the spiritual purpose is uppermost, through the infinite wisdom of God, buyer and seller will be brought together.

"An owner who desires to dispose of property should not feel that he is trying to be freed of a burden. He should know that God placed the property in his hands as a steward and that if his attitude is right toward it, the property is not burdensome to him. This realization will make clearer to him the real purpose which should underlie the sale."

Having released the property in thought, you should then work for a right connection. If there is only One Mind and we are all in It, we are always in touch with the person who needs what we have. It is divine Mind that brings us together. Get this realization, and you will not only attract the person who needs and wants what you have but who will pay the right price for it. What do we mean by the "right price"? We mean the price that you would be willing to pay for it yourself. If you ask more than it is worth or more than you would be willing to pay for it yourself, the law of justice and equity will not work.

How does Divine Mind locate this property and bring

the buyer to you? What is known in one part of Mind is known in all parts simultaneously. Contrary to the belief of many, the whole transaction takes place in mind. The Intelligence that offers the property for sale is the same Intelligence that leads the buyer to you. All you have to do is to remove the obstacles in your thought, and know that no circumstances, conditions, or persons can delay, hinder, or interfere with the sale in any way. Know that the deal is made, the money is in hand; see yourself turning this property over to the new owner; feel the happiness of both buyer and seller and share in the satisfaction the sale has produced.

"I AM NOW IN TOUCH WITH THE PERSON WHO NEEDS AND WANTS THIS PROPERTY AND CAN PAY THE RIGHT PRICE FOR IT."

29. PROSPERITY AND YOUR QUERIES

I.   IN FAITH I LOOK TO GOD FOR THE FULFILLMENT OF MY EVERY NEED.

Why are receiving and spending money an affirmation of our faith in God?

The act of receiving or spending money is an affirmation because money is a symbol of Universal supply. The words, "IN GOD WE TRUST," remind us to put our faith in the source of money (Spiritual Substance) rather than in the coin itself. The coin is but the outward and visible sign of an inward and spiritual Substance. It is well to think of these words whenever we receive or spend money. What does it mean to trust God? It means to rest confidently and expectantly in Him. When we trust God, we have a settled feeling about everything in our life. We know that there is always enough for our every need. Let us think of these words whenever we receive or spend money: "IN GOD WE TRUST." Let us think of them when our income has dwindled and our bills are unpaid. "IN GOD WE TRUST." Let us think of them when we are unemployed and our payments are overdue. Let us bless what we have and trust God for the rest.

II.   GOD SUBSTANCE FILLS MY MIND AND EVERYTHING I BLESS IS MULTIPLIED AND ENRICHED.

1. *Where* is *this formless God Substance to be found?*
   God Substance exists in the spiritual realm. It is all about us; it is in the very air we breathe.

2. *How does it take form?*
   It takes form through our thoughts, feelings, and words.

3. *How is a desire for greater manifestation fulfilled?*
   Greater manifestation comes through decrees. These are demands upon Universal Substance.

4. *How does a decree function?*
   It operates through the action of the conscious mind upon the subconscious acceptance of that which is asked for. A Mind Model held in this formless substance causes the idea to be created in form. First, comes the formation of the idea in thought; then the impression of the thought upon formless substance follows; and finally the creation results.

5. *How is the decree carried out?*
   It becomes manifest through words of blessing. Having made our decree, we carry it out by speaking words of blessing. We bless what we already have, what we desire to have, and what we expect to have, and it is quickened and increased.

III. THE RICHES OF GOD'S KINGDOM POUR THROUGH ME AND I AM ABUNDANTLY SUPPLIED.

1. *What is symbolized in the miracles of Changing the Water into Wine at the Wedding Feast of Cana, the Feeding of the Five Thousand, and the Draught of Fishes?*

   All these manifestations symbolize the Infinite riches of God's Kingdom.

2. *What is the purpose of these miracles?*

   They show that the multiplying power of Universal Substance is unlimited; they teach the means of laying hold of Divine Substance. When we have a problem of lack, we use the same means that Jesus used to multiply the loaves and fishes. First, we center our thought in the constant, abundant, and freely circulating God Substance. Second, we make our demand upon it (form a mental equivalent of our desire). Third, we impress this pattern upon the formless Substance through our faith and acceptance. Fourth, we give thanks for the fulfillment of our need. Fifth, we call the form forth through our faith. The riches of God's Kingdom are then manifested for us in abundant measure.

IV. MY PROSPERITY MANIFESTS BECAUSE I HAVE A COMPLETE ACCEPTANCE OF THE ETERNAL, OMNIPRESENT SUBSTANCE OF SPIRIT.

1. *What is the remedy for the conditions of poverty and lack?*

   We must enlarge our consciousness of Substance and increase our faith in God.

2. *Why is it that some people live in perpetual limitation and want?*

   They possess a belief that they can never be rich.

3. *Why can a negative mind not produce wealth and success?*

   A negative mind is a non-productive and non-creative mind. The negative mind inhibits, scatters, and obstructs all of the desirable things.

4. *Why is the mind more important in demonstrating prosperity than the hands?*

   The mind governs and works through the hands. Everything in the Universe began as an idea of the mind; if the mind and hands of a man do not move in the same direction, he will never get rich. He will, so to speak, be short-circuiting the power that can make him prosperous.

5. *What should one do if one's supply of money is insufficient for his needs?*

The first thing to do is to drop all worry and fear. The second thing is to turn attention to God. The third thing is to recognize that God's Substance is here now.

30. PROSPERITY AND RESENTMENT

"HE THAT IS SLOW TO WRATH IS OF GREAT
UNDERSTANDING."

There is no quicker way to drive away your prosperity than by a festering resentment. It is pitiful to hear poor people blaming their fate on social injustices, bad luck, and greedy employers, when the real problem is their inability to handle the negative and resentful thoughts in their minds. They do not realize that they were mental paupers to begin with and that they can never hope to change their condition nor to get the things they want until they make room for them in their consciousness. It is natural to want something better than we have, but the way to get it is not to berate others. We get what we want when we let go of the things that keep it out of our lives.

Resentment is what the word implies – *re-sent-ment*. It is sending evil back to a person whom we imagine has injured us. It is not only a destructive and punitive thought, but it is also highly emotional. Where does resentment come from? It comes from a sensitive, touchy, uncontrolled, unsurrendered, and undisciplined ego. The resentful person is a fearful, hostile, lonely, and rejected person. He is afraid because he is alone, and he is hostile because he is afraid. A controlled ego is impervious to hurt; an uncontrolled ego is ravaged by it.

Charles Beaudelaire says: "Hatred is a precious liquor,

a poison dearer than all the Borgias, because it is made of our blood, our health, our sleep, and two thirds of our love." If I were asked, "What is the greatest single cause of failure, frustration, and defeat in human life?", I should answer without fear of contradiction, "Resentment." The resentful person must face this question: Does my resentment accomplish anything? Elsie Robinson answered this question when she said, "Even if our rage seems fully justified, and our plans succeed beyond our blackest hope, we will never get even, for life doesn't work that way. Instead of finding peace, renewed self respect, and healing from our heart, each attempt at revenge leaves us frustrated, cheated. Instead of punishing our enemies, we've simply played our debasing game and sold ourselves down the river."

There are thousands of reasons why no one can afford to resent or hate anybody or anything, but one of the chief ones is that it throws everything in the body out of balance and has a crushing effect upon the brain.

"But I have a right," you say, "to resent the people who have injured me." That is true. But you also have the right to drink carbolic acid. The result is the same. You have the right to hold animosities, spites, and hates; but if you exercise your right to resent, it is slow suicide. The smart thing to do is to call the roll of those toward whom you are inclined to feel resentful and not only forgive them but pray for them. Never discuss the things you dislike about a person, but talk always about the things you do like. Make your agreement with disagreements at once. Have *"the peace that passeth all understanding"* and all misunderstanding, as well. Be too big to hate anybody or anything. Develop a skin so tough that you won't even know when you are being insulted or hurt.

"I SAY UNTO YOU, THAT YE RESIST NOT EVIL."

31. PROSPERITY AND SAVING

"YE KNOW NOT WHAT SHALL BE ON THE MORROW."

When the metaphysician urges saving as a means to prosperity, he is thinking chiefly of the psychological effect upon the saver. The effect of saving is purely metaphysical. It gives an upward trend to the mind, stimulates self-confidence, and arouses enthusiasm. It also eliminates fear and worry, and these emotions are at the root of most financial difficulties. The moment a man begins to save systematically, he becomes a happier and more contented man. He begins to feel a sense of release, security, and freedom. The consciousness of a little nest egg gives him a sense of power and protection. He has taken the first step toward financial independence and the development of a sturdy character. Theodore Roosevelt once said, "If you would be sure that you are beginning right, begin to save. The habit of saving money while it stiffens the will also brightens the energies."

Now, let us take a quick look at the subject of hoarding. Jesus speaks of the *"deceitfulness of riches."* St. Paul says that *"The love of money is the root of all evil."* How can money be both good and evil? By the use we make of it. Now hold that word *love* for a moment. St. Paul is saying that the man who loves money more than the Source is limiting the money he has. Money can bring trouble as well as peace. It can bring care instead of ease. It can bring pain instead of pleasure. It can bring sorrow instead of happiness. No one can feel prosperous or secure who is living from hand to mouth. We all need a reserve for emergencies, constructive purposes, the unforeseen needs, but let us make sure that the motive in our saving is right. Let us make sure that it does not become an end in itself. If our saving is for a reasonable provision for future needs, it is quite a different thing from money hoarded for a rainy day. People who save for rainy days create the days they are trying to guard against.

The important thing in saving is a constructive motive and a definite purpose for what we put aside. Money stored as a happiness fund brings ease, confidence, comfort, and protection; money saved from fear or dread of future calamity brings trouble, disaster, and misery. There is a fine point here, and it is important that you get it. If you have a job, it is always easier to get another one. If you have some money, it is always easier to get more. Why is this true? Because "Like attracts like" and "Like begets like." The reason it is hard for a rich man to get into the Kingdom of Heaven is that he loves riches more than the Source.

"LAY NOT UP FOR YOURSELVES TREASURES UPON EARTH WHERE MOTH AND DUST DOTH CORRUPT, AND WHERE THIEVES BREAK THROUGH AND STEAL; BUT LAY UP FOR YOURSELVES TREASURES IN HEAVEN. FOR

WHERE YOUR TREASURE IS, THERE WILL YOUR HEART BE ALSO."

32. Prosperity and Security

1. KEEP A RECORD OF WHAT YOU SPEND. Know where your money goes. Keep an accurate account of everything you spend for at least thirty days.

2. MAKE AN AIR-TIGHT BUDGET. This will not only cut down your financial worries but will give you a sense of financial and emotional security. If you do not know how to make a budget, get the help of your banker or some social agency in your city. If they cannot help you, call your newspaper, the Red Cross, or the Community Chest.

3. LEARN HOW TO GET THE MOST FOR YOUR MONEY. There are many Government Bulletins that will give you this information. They will help you see why some people get more for their money than others.

4. DO BUSINESS WITH YOUR BANK. If you must borrow to meet an emergency, go to a bank and not to a loan shark. The latter will complicate your life and make you miserable.

5. CARRY LIFE INSURANCE. It is not only your greatest protection against death, sickness, and emergencies, but is also one of your finest assets. Make sure, however, that your Insurance Policy

has a savings or cash value.

6. If your Life Insurance Policy is for the protection of your wife and children, put it in a Trust Fund. Do not have it paid to your wife in cash.

7. BUY A HOME OF YOUR OWN. There are those who will tell you that it is cheaper to pay rent, but it isn't. Buying a home is like putting money in a bank. It gives you a sense of comfort and security that no other material possession does.

8. MAKE A WILL. Determine beforehand who is to receive your personal effects and securities. A will saves time and expense and obviates much bickering and quarreling after you have gone.

9. PAY YOUR BILLS WHEN THEY ARE DUE. Holding what belongs to another seriously affects your income. It causes lack of circulation and stagnation. Remember that you are a distributor of God's wealth and not a terminal. Money is not yours to hold but to circulate.

10. DO NOT GAMBLE. If you are tempted to gamble, read *How to Figure the Odds* by Oswald Jacoby. The odds are always against you.

11. INVEST IN DEPENDABLE SECURITIES. The important thing when investing money is to know the people with whom you are doing business. If you do not have this information, go to a reputable

Bond House or Bank. Perfect safety is more important than large returns.

12. GIVE TO OTHERS. The real purpose in giving money to people is to make them independent and self-reliant. Make sure, therefore, that your giving does not pauperize or weaken. More important than giving money is showing people how to help themselves. Every metaphysical student should also be a missionary.

"DIVINE LOVE BOUNTIFULLY SUPPLIES AND INCREASES SUBSTANCE TO MEET MY EVERY NEED."

33. PROSPERITY AND SELF-FAITH

"HAVE THE FAITH OF GOD."

"I am the greatest Power in the world. I was with Jesus when He healed the sick, raised the dead, walked on the water, opened the tomb, turned water into wine, stilled the storm, and fed the five thousand. I was with Lindberg when he flew the Atlantic, with Madame Curie when she discovered radium, with Cyrus Field when he laid the ocean cable, with Pasteur when he discovered vaccine, with Edison when he invented the electric light, with Alexander Graham Bell when he perfected the telephone, with Livingstone when he went into darkest Africa. I am with all those who do the things that cannot be done. I am the power that moves mountains of difficulties, uncovers secrets, lightens burdens, penetrates mysteries, heals disease, spans rivers, opens heaven, solves problems, demagnetizes evil, purifies consciousness, balances life, clarifies vision, destroys ignorance, builds fortunes, overcomes lack, demonstrates riches, strengthens purpose, gives direction, empowers thought, fulfills desire, stimulates income. I am a friend to all men and an enemy to none. I am a go-getter, producer, booster, and an optimist. I recognize no barrier, limitation, or obstacle. I know no defeat. I always get what I go after. I succeed when everyone else fails. I overcome every adverse condition and conquer all difficulties.

I accomplish everything I set out to do. I AM SELF-FAITH."

Faith! What a mighty and stupendous word it is! *"If ye have faith as a grain of mustard seed, ye shall say unto this mountain, Remove hence to yonder place; and it shall remove; and nothing shall be impossible unto you."* Faith is the cup we hold up to the Universe to be filled. It is the measure of our acceptance and belief. We receive what we ask. A one-talent man with great faith in himself will attract infinitely more than a ten-talent man with no faith. It makes no difference whether your ambition is to build a great industry, to accumulate vast resources, to amass fabulous riches, or to win a high place in your field, the one indispensable and imperative thing is an unwavering and immovable faith in yourself. If you have it, then no circumstance or combination of circumstances can ever defeat you.

Are you discouraged? Are you ready to give up? Remember that it is the last blow that splits the rock. *"If God be for us, who can be against us?"* *"Greater is he that is in you than he that is in the world."* Say these statements over and over to yourself until they become integrated with the creative forces of your subconscious mind. They will stimulate your self-faith as nothing else will. It is not your puny little faith that you are seeking to use but God's Faith. Jesus said, *"Have the faith of God."* In other words, "Get some of God's faith and then when you have that, you will have the power with which mountains can be removed and cast into the sea."

It is not our faith that does the impossible and the unreasonable but God's faith. St. Paul said, *"For I say, through the grace given unto me, to every man that is among you, not to think of himself more highly than he ought to think; but to think soberly AS GOD HAS DEALT TO EVERY MAN THE MEASURE OF FAITH."* Where is this faith to be born? In the heart (subconscious mind).

Then what about the failures? There are no failures except those who admit failure. The law says that "Like attracts like." The world accepts a man at his own evaluation. If he fails, it is because he has lost faith in himself. It is because he has waited for luck, pull, influence, or outside capital to give him a boost. *"Faith without works is dead."* A man must not only have faith in his ability, but must also have the energy to put his ability to work. Faith and works go hand in hand. "No man ever climbed to success on another man's shoulders."

"THE FATHER THAT DWELLETH IN ME, HE DOETH THE WORKS."

34. PROSPERITY AND SORROW

"MINE EYE IS CONSUMED BECAUSE OF GRIEF."

It is our purpose in this lesson to show that grief and sorrow not only produce sickness and disease in the body but also loss and disintegration in the purse or material possessions. But first, let us inquire into the nature of sorrow. The dictionary defines it this way: "Uneasiness or pain of mind due to loss or disappointment: unhappiness, sadness." Who is there who has not shared this emotion? Sorrow speaks a common language and comes to all alike. It is in fact the most certain of all human afflictions.

There are many causes of sorrow, but the greatest cause is death. We believe that death is the gateway to a larger and fuller life, but we meet it with black raiment, armlets, ties, floral tributes, mournful music, paroxysms of pain, morbid grief, elaborate rituals, and costly trappings. What is wrong with this picture? We have our grief in reverse. Now be frank with yourself. Think of the heart aches, failures, disappointments, misery, sufferings, and tragedies of the living. Wouldn't it be more Christian and more sensible if we regarded the deceased with joy and happiness rather than with sorrow and gloom? If one must grieve, the logical time for grieving is the birth of an infant.

The only way that sorrow can operate in our lives is through our attitudes, thoughts, feelings, and emotions. We make our sorrow by sad thoughts, painful memories, and self-pity; we unmake it by reversing our thoughts. The cause of our suffering is not in the things that happen to us, but in our reaction to them. It is the reaction that determines the result. Remember that. We are not dealing with death, separation, and loss but with our thoughts about death, separation, and loss. When we stop feeding our sorrow with self-pity and morbidity, the sorrow will quickly heal. The cure lies in our ability to transfer our attention from self to others.

Socrates said, "He that grieves much is a magnet to attract waste of property." Why does grief affect our material possessions, income, and finances? Because it is a belief in separation and loss. Grief not only causes deterioration of the body and personality but disorganization of the whole life. Fear may be the most destructive emotion, but grief is the most wasteful. It wastes energy, impairs efficiency, and withers the soul. To grieve over the passing of a loved one is natural, but to capitulate to grief is cowardly. Did you ever ask yourself what would happen if there were no death? There would be no room for oncoming generations. One generation gives way to another. Death comes to all alike. Whether it makes or breaks us depends upon our attitude toward it.

The first step in overcoming our sorrow is to prepare ourselves for its coming. This preparation should be made when life is smooth, sweet, and pleasant. How? By building into our lives faith, hope, confidence, self-control, intellectual poise, and a re-assuring hope of immortality. We must not only surrender our sorrow into God's hands, but we must occupy ourselves with some constructive and useful work for others. We must use our sorrow instead of wasting it. Since the loss of a loved one by death is a universal experience, we should not be surprised when the experience comes to us. If our love for the departed one is real, we shall make him happy by being happy ourselves. He has earned his new-found joy, and we must not hamper him in his onward way.

Albert Cliffe says: "If we could but see with our spiritual eyes our church at the time of Holy Communion we should, I am certain, see it filled with those who have passed on to that Great Beyond – joining with us in Christian fellowship – celebrating with us His sacramental service. A glorious reunion for every one of you if you will only believe."

35. PROSPERITY AND STEWARDSHIP

"GIVE AN ACCOUNT OF THY STEWARDSHIP."

When we know the Law of Giving and Receiving, we know that we never get anything for nothing. Jesus placed great emphasis on stewardship. There are twenty-nine parables in the New Testament, and thirteen of them deal with the right use of money. Why is the subject so important? Because a man's stewardship (capacity to give) is the acid test of his sincerity and faith in God. If he is unwilling to give, he cannot hope to receive. The Certain Rich Man, whose story is told by St. Luke, failed to meet this test just as so many do today. People spend billions on alcohol, cosmetics, cigarettes, jewelry, perfume, and theatres; but when it comes to church and community enterprises, they give as little as possible. When will we learn that life uses the same measure that we use? *"With the same measure ye mete* [that you use], *it shall be measured to you again."* The stingy man closes his channels of supply; the generous man opens them.

But you say: "I am having tough sledding. Everything is going against me; I have lost my faith in God and in everything else." Be careful, my friend. You are complicating your problem instead of helping it. You have your Principle in reverse. You are creating poverty instead of prosperity. Be honest with yourself. How much of your income have you given to the support of God's work and to the relief of human suffering? Would it be less than ten per cent? Then you are robbing God.

It is a sad commentary on our religious training that so many people try to get something for nothing. Their attitude toward sharing is one of evasion and indifference, and their excuse is that religion should be free. Of course, religion is free. Water is free, too, but it takes money to pump it to your home. *"Give and it shall be given unto you."* That Law is woven into the very fabric of human life. Those who neglect it do so at their peril; it is the failure to keep this Law that results in much of the misery, poverty, sickness, and unhappiness in the world. Those who seek spiritual blessings and expect only to receive will never realize them.

Jesus was very clear on this point. When He sent his disciples out to preach the gospel, He sent them without script or purse. Why? Because He expected those to whom they ministered to support them and to take care of their material needs. If the people of the city did not do this, the disciples were told to shake the dust of that city off their feet.

The same situation exists today. If a minister, teacher, or practitioner is to be helpful and effective in his ministrations, he must be relieved of all financial care. It is not his duty to make the church or spiritual organization strong, but ours. We should give not from the top of our purse but from the depths of our heart. We are the channels through which God supports His ministers, teachers, and healers. It is a

poor rule that does not work both ways. If we have not been
healed, let us look to our stewardship. Let us find wherein WE
have failed.

>*"BY AN EQUALITY THAT NOW AT THIS TIME
>YOUR ABUNDANCE MAY BE A SUPPLY FOR
>THEIR WANT, THAT THEIR ABUNDANCE ALSO
>MAY BE A SUPPLY FOR YOUR WANT."*

>*"I GIVE AS I EXPECT TO RECEIVE."*

36. PROSPERITY AND STRAIN

"THE MORROW SHALL TAKE THOUGHT FOR THE THINGS OF ITSELF."

If you tabulate the obituary notices in your daily paper, you will be impressed by the fact that most of the men who die in their early forties and fifties are the aggressive, dynamic, progressive, go-getters. They are the men of achievement, vigor, and action. They are the top-notchers who have something on the ball: dynamic men, forceful men, energetic men, worried men, anxious men, crowded men, hurried men, over-extended men, strained men – dead men. But why? Why do so many break down and go to pieces? Why the number who die of hypertension diseases? Because the pressure of living beats them to pieces inside. There is no quiet in their souls. They are filled with hurry, worry, friction, and strain which the body cannot stand.

On the human side, it gives us a sense of pride to be referred to as a "human dynamo"; but it is the human dynamos nowadays who are always burned out when they are needed most.

Perhaps you are one of the persons who are right now riding on the rims and headed for the shelf. Why don't you have a check-up and find out? It is good practice, and it may save your life. If you find that you are a bridge-crosser, do something about it. Find out if you are living in the present or in the future. You can meet all the problems that can be crowded into one day, but you cannot carry tomorrow's load with today's energy. Be frank with yourself. Are you mentally crowded, worried, fearful, hurried, and overburdened? The mind goes to pieces under the impact of such thoughts. CHANGE YOUR MIND. Are you all wound up? Then let go. Unwind. The surest way to eliminate strain is to live one day at a time. It is all that your heart and your mind can carry with safety. Do one thing at a time. Breakdowns come from lack of reserve power. *"Be still and know."* Relax and let go. You need the peace, poise, power, and balance that come with silence and stillness. Practice periods of stillness many times a day.

Everyone should hold a silence and meditation at least once a day. Go by yourself for fifteen or twenty minutes and contemplate the Divine Presence as supply. Seat yourself in a straight-backed chair, close your eyes, and relax your body from head to foot. Meditate upon some such prosperity statement as these: *"I and the Father are one."* "I inherit the wealth of the universe and it eagerly and actively seeks me out, pouring its great wealth upon me. The riches of God's Kingdom flood my whole being."

Then image the thing you want and ask God for it. Know that you have received what you have asked and continue to give thanks for it until the desire is fulfilled.

Eliminate the waste of noise. A noisy life is an

impotent life. A disturbed life is an uncertain life. Noisy voices indicate shallow thoughts. If you would live a long, healthy, and prosperous life, tune out the voices and enervating noises within you. Make haste slowly. "Green fruit is never sweet." Wealth that is not related to your consciousness brings disappointment, failure, and humiliation in its wake. Anxiety and haste delay the manifestation of your good. *"He that hasteth to be rich hath an evil eye, and considereth not that poverty shall come upon him."* But he that goes along with God in the realization of his abundance shall in due time receive his own. Do not try to rush the season or to force the crop. *"BE STILL AND KNOW THAT I AM GOD."* When you make a demand on the Universe. assume that it has been fulfilled. Do not dig up the earth to see if the seed is growing. Do not seek confirmation of your faith. Worry and uncertainty about the outcome of your treatment are unconscious attempts to force your good. Concern is a lack of trust. Live by indirection; live laborlessly. Think without anxiety. Pray without effort. These are the secrets of a long, full, happy, useful, and rich life. When your work is done in consciousness, the answer is assured.

"PEACE I LEAVE WITH YOU, MY PEACE I GIVE UNTO YOU: NOT AS THE WORLD GIVETH GIVE I UNTO YOU. LET NOT YOUR HEART BE TROUBLED, NEITHER LET IT BE AFRAID."

37. PROSPERITY AND SUPPLY

"MY GOD SHALL SUPPLY ALL YOUR NEED."

In the Feeding of the Five Thousand, recorded in all four Gospels, we have a striking example of the power of Substance to multiply and increase itself. The disciples are face to face with a desperate situation. There were five thousand hungry people on hand to be fed. What could they do in such a situation? They did what you and I would probably have done. They took an inventory of their assets and stated the result: *"There is a lad here which hath five barley loaves. and two small fishes: but what are they among so many?"* Does that sound familiar? "I have here but fifty dollars, and I need five hundred." "I have here only enough food to run me for a week." "I have nothing to give. "I have nothing to wear," And so on, and so on. Are these things true? How about your God? Don't you believe in Him? Has He ever turned His back on you? Has He ever refused anything you asked? Has He ever disappointed you? Is it not possible that right now He can meet this need for you? Was Jesus worried about feeding the five thousand hungry persons who had *"run afoot thither out of all cities"* to learn of Him? Remember that the day was *"far spent"* and they were in *"a desert place."* St. John tells us that He was not worried or anxious, for *"He Himself knew what He would do."* What a heartening realization this is even today! The disciples sought to send the people away, but Jesus

said, *"They need not depart; give ye them to eat."* He had a
plan and He was going to carry it out. *"They need not depart"*
because He was adequate to their need. The Christ is always
adequate to our needs. He is the same yesterday, today, and
forever. He fulfills our needs now just as He did then. *"And
they did all eat, and were filled. And they took up twelve
baskets full of the fragments, and of the fishes." "I have
planted, Apollos watered, but God gave the increase."* All
human needs are fulfilled by cooperating with God and not by
magnifying our poverty. The wise man takes into account the
spiritual forces as well as the material.

Why is this demonstration commonly called a miracle?
Because for centuries the materialist has believed that it
transcends natural law. The metaphysician, however, knows
that it is wholly in accord with Divine Principle. Jesus was
able to feed five thousand people with five loaves and two
small fishes through His knowledge that Universal Substance
has power to increase and multiply itself. What is the promise
in this story for us? God has given us the same power to
materialize Substance that Jesus had. Rich ideas circulating
through our consciousness cause prosperity to be attracted to
us. They build up such an awareness of abundance that there is
no longer any room for a single idea of lack. When the
disciples replaced their belief in lack with ideas of abundance,
the truth was fulfilled.

"I REFUSE TO ACKNOWLEDGE THE APPEARANCE OF LACK. I AFFIRM THAT THE CONTINUAL AND INEXHAUSTIBLE SUBSTANCE OF GOD IS MANIFESTED IN MY LIFE NOW."

38. PROSPERITY AND TAXES

"AND ALL WENT TO BE TAXED."

Do you complain, groan, and resent your taxes, dues, and other obligations? Perhaps you need a new perspective. Someone has clearly stated the point of view: "Taxes are the price we pay for living in a democracy. If you think the price is high, let us look around us at the large part of the world ridden by dictators. One such look will surely convince us that we are getting a great deal for our money."

Good Business in the March, 1944 issue presented an "Income Tax Blessing", by Charles E. Gilbert, that is well worth our attention.

"I bless this income tax form.

"I bless the Federal government which asks for this tax. I bless this land which has given me my chance to earn this income. I bless the laws of this land which have guided and protected me and my fellow men and my family while I earned this income.

"I bless this income tax form with its seeming complications. I declare that it is not too complicated for me to fill out accurately. I bless my fellow men who arranged the items on the form. The divine wisdom that guided them in preparing the form is guiding me in making my computations.

"I bless the income that has come to me through the year. I bless and set down every item as the substance of Spirit that has been provided for me. I have returned a part to the Lord as an expression of gratitude to Him for His kindness to me. I have been glad to make this return to Him. I gladly make the required return to my United States also, in gratitude for the privileges it has given me.

"I bless the deductions and the exemptions I am allowed. When I compute these I deal honestly with my Lord and with my government. I see these deductions as evidence that my government is considerate and reasonable in its requirements.

"I bless the actual taxes that I shall pay. When the time comes to pay the taxes, the Lord will provide the means whereby I can meet the obligation.

"I bless all who shall handle these taxes. I bless the taxes for their part in supplying my country's needs; therefore, I bless my country itself. May righteousness, justice, good will, and peace prevail throughout all its actions at home and abroad! May divine wisdom guide its officials and its citizens! May victory come to us and our allies! May the benefits that we enjoy in this country of freedom and prosperity and brotherhood be extended to all parts of the world, and may war be known no more on the face of the earth."

39. Prosperity and Thanksgiving

"WITH THANKSGIVING, LET YOUR REQUESTS BE MADE KNOWN UNTO GOD." "IN EVERYTHING, GIVE THANKS."

It is our purpose in this study to give you an infallible method of demonstration. It will not only produce new ideas and increase your power of attraction, but give you the means whereby your problems can be solved and your desires and wishes can be fulfilled. It is such a simple formula that a child can use it with success. It is asking, believing, and receiving all in one law – The Law of Thanksgiving. Thanksgiving is like yeast in bread. It is the active quality in our consciousness that not only increases supply but solves every problem in our lives. Gratitude keeps the mind in balance and makes it strong, one-pointed, and true. It feeds our hopes, strengthens our faith, nourishes our aspirations, and causes abundance to become manifest in our affairs. In reality, it is the great harmonizer and unifier between ourselves and God. *"In everything, give thanks."*

"The whole process of mental adjustment and atonement can be summed up in the one word: *gratitude,"* says Wallace D. Wattles in *Financial Success Through Creative Thought.* "Many people who order their lives rightly in all other ways are kept in poverty by their lack of gratitude.

The grateful outreaching of your mind in thankful praise to the Supreme Being is a liberation or expenditure of force; it cannot fail to reach that to which it is addressed, and the reaction is an instantaneous movement toward you." That is a strong statement, but anyone can prove it for himself.

If the author were asked to name the most important emotion in demonstrating prosperity, he would say, "Gratitude." Why? Because gratitude is the only channel through which the desired good can come into our lives. What is the great and only problem in demonstrating supply? To unify our minds with the Universal Substance so that it becomes receptive and responsive to our thoughts. How is this problem solved? Through a whole-souled and continuous feeling of deep gratitude. It is only when we fail to obey the Law of Thanksgiving that limited and negative conditions arise.

If there is such a thing as a short cut to demonstration, it is to be found in the prayer of thanksgiving. Genuine gratitude opens the entire being to God; it lifts us above the material plane where poverty, want, sickness, and other negative conditions hold sway. Whenever we lift our hearts in thanksgiving, we free the mind from the undesirable, negative thoughts that prevent our acceptance of the things for which we have prayed.

If we had the space, we should like to give you some of the case histories of discouraged persons whose good did not begin to move until they made the Prayer of Thanksgiving their own. Then their diseases were healed, their problems were solved, and their desires were fulfilled. The reason for their failure was their bondage to the material plane; God's gifts could not get through to them.

The Bible tells us that we must give thanks for everything. Does that mean the bad as well as the good? It certainly does. We should give thanks for happiness, health, home, family, love, peace, truth, understanding, food, clothing, sleep, and money. We should thank God when we spend money, give money away, or when we pay our bills. We should also give thanks when we receive money because we recognize it as coming from the Divine Source. We should give thanks for the adversities, disciplines, trials, tribulations, problems, and unpleasant experiences that test our mettle. Why should we give thanks for the stern experiences of life? There are two reasons: Giving thanks takes the sting out of the unpleasant things, and helps us to make our agreement with them.

Let the words that follow be your first thought in the morning and your last thought at night; as surely as the sun rises, God's blessings will pour in upon you.

"I AM GRATEFUL FOR THIS DAY AND FOR THE CHANCE TO PROVE MY DOMINION OVER EVERY PROBLEM IT MAY BRING."

40. PROSPERITY AND TITHING

"SEE THAT YE ABOUND IN THIS GRACE, ALSO."

Any system that has endured and proved itself for centuries demands our utmost consideration. Tithing is not a popular subject even in religious circles because people do not understand it. The proof of the pudding, as we say, is in the eating. If millions acclaim tithing as the true basis of prosperity, we need to do some serious thinking about it.

In the old dispensation, the tithe (tenth) was not only the portion to be returned to the Lord (Law), but it was a way of acknowledging God as the Source of all Supply. It was never considered as a contribution, compensation, charity, gift, or reward, but as a thank offering for blessings received. It was returned to the Source in the same way that the farmer returns the best seed to the soil.

Tithing preserves the contact between man and his Source. It keeps his purse in contact with Universal Supply. *"Thou shalt truly tithe all the increase of thy seed."* The Law says that ten per cent of your income belongs to the Source, and to fail to return it is to rob God. When the tithe has been turned back to the Source (Law), the spiritual benefits are assured, for the Law of Prosperity is perpetuated in your affairs.

Why is tithing the true basis of Prosperity? Giving with most people is accompanied by a false sense of separation or loss. Tithing is true giving, that is, sharing. It recognizes our dependence upon God for supply. It develops an opulent consciousness, which is the secret of continuous and automatic income. The soul that does not give shrivels.

How is the tithe to be given? Joyously, hilariously, and cheerfully. If we give with a sense of compulsion, it is like planting vegetable seeds and neglecting to water or cultivate them.

When is the tithe to be given? *"Upon the first day of the week."* What is the tithe? The tithe is ten per cent of all that you receive or, according to St. Paul, *"as you may prosper."* Ten per cent is the minimum. The tithe by putting God first in our finances is the solution to all our problems of supply.

What are the benefits of tithing? It keeps mean, stingy, fearful, and limited thoughts out of the mind and keeps the good flowing in.

To what is the tithe to be given? It is to be given to God's work, or to that specific organization through which you receive your spiritual help. By God's work is meant work that puts man in possession of himself and enables him to live the victorious life of Christ, the life of freedom, health, prosperity, service, joy, generosity, power, and efficiency.

"As ye abound in everything, in faith, and utterance, and knowledge, and in all diligence, and in your love to us, see that ye abound in this grace also."

"Honor the Lord with thy substance, and the first fruits of all thine increase: So shall thy barns be filled with plenty, and thy presses shall burst out with new wine."

"OF THE INCREASE THAT LIFE GIVES TO ME, I RETURN ONE TENTH TO MY SOURCE. THIS TENTH IS IN MY HAND FOR THE MOMENT AS ITS STEWARD. RETURNING IT IMMEDIATELY TO ITS SOURCE, I KEEP AN UNBROKEN CIRCUIT OF CREATIVE POWER FLOWING THROUGH ME, MY BUSINESS, AND MY FINANCES."

41. Prosperity and Understanding

"HE THAT IS PERFECT IN KNOWLEDGE IS WITH THEE."

Those who would seek to demonstrate a large supply will do well to listen to Solomon: *"Happy is the man that findeth wisdom, and the man that getteth understanding, for the merchandise of it is better than the merchandise of silver, and the gain thereof of fine gold. She is more precious than rubies: and all the things thou canst desire are not to be compared unto her."*

Solomon was not only the richest man of his time but also the wisest. He did not lean upon the perishable symbols of silver and gold but upon the substance of true ideas in Mind. Why did he say that understanding was more productive than silver and gold? Because understanding is both the Consciousness and Substance of all things, whereas money is only the effect, or shadow of substance.

Jesus understood this truth perfectly; He never looked outside of His Consciousness for anything. His Consciousness was both *"the substance of things hoped for"* and *"the evidence of things not seen."* Because He understood that He and the Father were One, His Consciousness was an automatic and continuous source of supply. When we understand that the prayer (desire) and the answer (fulfillment) are both in Mind, we shall understand why Jesus said, *"What things soever ye desire, when ye pray believe that ye receive them and ye shall have them."*

If man is Mind, as Jesus taught, the awareness of a desire is equivalent to its fulfillment. It is the Mind that entertains the desire and the Mind that fulfills it. *"With all thy getting, get understanding."* Understanding of what? Understanding that we are dependent upon ideas for our prosperity rather than upon money. If God is ALL GOOD, there can be no lack of good for those who know God and apply His Laws. If God is Omnipresent Substance, there can be no lack of Substance in our affairs (our jobs – our professions – our stores – our firms – our welfare – our bodies – everything in our lives).

H. Emilie Cady says: "There is only God through and through and through all things, in our bodies, in our seemingly empty purses, in our circumstances, just waiting that invisible substance for us to recognize and acknowledge HIM and HIM alone in order to become visible. All else is a lie."

The only true prosperity is a Prosperity Consciousness. Supply does not come *out* of it; it is permanently *within* it. Poverty is simply a gap in consciousness. To close the gap, we must demonstrate Consciousness instead of money. We must see prosperity as an effect and not as a cause. We must see it as an idea in Mind and realize that we can never be separated from it. The idea demonstrates and supports itself; when we grasp this concept, we shall see why Solomon told us to get understanding.

"All things are yours," said Jesus. How does one get this realization? By getting a clear picture of the desire and by holding to it through thick and thin. Be careful, however, that you do not outline or place a monetary value on it. If your demonstration depends upon a sum of money and the money does not materialize, the demonstration cannot be made. The better way is to get the feeling of the fulfillment of your desire.

"LENGTH OF DAYS IS IN HER [WISDOM'S] RIGHT HAND AND IN HER LEFT HAND RICHES AND HONOUR. HER WAYS ARE WAYS OF PLEASANTNESS, AND ALL HER PATHS ARE PEACE. SHE IS A TREE OF LIFE TO THEM THAT LAY HOLD UPON HER; AND HAPPY IS EVERYONE THAT RETAINETH HER."

42. PROSPERITY AND VALUES – I
(Deceitfulness of Riches)

"NO MAN CAN SERVE TWO MASTERS. EITHER HE WILL HATE THE ONE AND LOVE THE OTHER, OR HE WILL HOLD TO THE ONE AND DESPISE THE OTHER. YE CANNOT SERVE GOD AND MAMMON."

All through the centuries, what Jesus referred to as *"the deceitfulness of riches, and the lusts of other things,"* has produced a great share of sorrow in the lives of men and nations. We are indebted to Dr. John W. Holland for an article that appeared in a recent issue of "The Challenge." It carries a message for every person, rich or poor, but is particularly pertinent for those whose ambition is to have great possessions.

"We Americans, Christian and un-Christian alike, have over-stressed the value of material things…We learned to express all values in dollars. We had no titled nobility, so we created one out of the people who had gotten together vast wealth. But in times of financial stress our material gods did not save us.

"In 1923 a group of the world's most successful financiers met at the Edgewater Beach Hotel in Chicago. Present were: (a) the president of the largest independent steel company; (b) the president of the largest independent utility company; (c) the world's greatest wheat speculator; (d) the president of the New York Stock Exchange; (e) a member of the President's Cabinet; (f) the greatest 'bear' in Wall Street; (g) the president of the Bank of International Settlements; (h) the head of the world's greatest monopoly; (i) the president of the largest gas company.

"It is said that these men controlled more wealth than there was in the United States Treasury. For years our magazines and some of our pulpits were holding up these 'financially successful' men as samples to American Youth. Years passed – came 1948 – what happened to these men?

"The president of the largest steel company lived on borrowed money for the last five years of his life.

"The greatest wheat speculator died abroad, insolvent.

"The president of the New York Stock Exchange was recently released from Sing Sing Prison.

"The member of the President's Cabinet was pardoned from prison that he might die at home.

"The greatest 'bear' in Wall Street committed suicide.

"The president of the Bank of International Settlements committed suicide.

"The head of the world's greatest monopoly committed suicide.

"The president of the world's largest gas company became insane.

"These men were not sinners above others. They had

simply lived for earth, and when that part of the earth which they had gained slipped from their hands, there was nothing left to prop up their courage.

"Those who are in a position to know whereof they speak will tell you that many worshippers of Mammon have committed suicide who were reported to have died natural deaths. Their families succeeded in having the manner of their going kept quiet.

"Nor were those mentioned the only rich men who have gone to jail. Certainly they were not the only ones who ought to have gone but who escaped the wrath of man. Yet they and all others of their kind can never escape the sure result of their worship of the golden calf, even though they endow many libraries and hospitals as monuments to themselves. Under the working of Divine Law, they must reap the result of their so-called success, though the reaping be done in the world to come."

"IF RICHES INCREASE, SET NOT YOUR HEART UPON THEM...POWER BELONGETH UNTO GOD."

43. Prosperity and Values – II

If we can show you that depressions and business slumps are purely psychological, we can show you how to rise above them. In the great depression of 1929, we suffered not so much from a decline in values as from a decline in man's thoughts. Everybody was trying to get rid of stocks because their values were going down. Why were they going down? Had the values of the properties and the holdings of sound companies and corporations changed? Was the telephone service discontinued? Did railroads stop running? Were automobile plants shut down? No. Then what happened? Why the crash? Why did everything go to pieces? Because of man's fear. The decline was purely psychological. Then where did all the money go? Why has it now reappeared? Because of another change in man's thought. Stocks have now assumed a new value in his mind.

Do you see what we are trying to bring out? The value of a thing depends entirely upon the Law of Demand and Supply. If the demand is great, the value is high. If the demand is small, the value is low. It is just like a bone in the back yard which your dog has ceased to gnaw. If another dog comes along and takes the bone, your dog wants it back again right away. So man tends to value highly the thing that others want.

The reason values change is that the thoughts of man change. If every stockholder were happy with his stocks and wanted to keep them, the market would be stable and prices would begin to rise. But fear creeps into the picture. We lose our heads and sacrifice the thing we have because we think that others do not want it.

Don't you see that stock market jitters like all other problems are purely psychological and must be dealt with in the mind? What is the most necessary and least appreciated thing in human life? Water. If water should suddenly begin to disappear from the face of the earth, it would immediately become the most valuable thing in every household. We would gladly exchange anything we had for it. Perhaps we should re-appraise the things that God has provided so lavishly for us; we may find that we should place a higher value upon them.

If the cause of financial panics, bank failures, and poverty is fear, we need to cultivate faith and confidence in the permanence, power, and reality of God's invisible and omnipresent Good. Let us not get panicky over the rise and decline of particular forms of good because they seem scarce. Let us not lose our heads because others are losing theirs. Let us hold fast to those spiritual values that do not change. Let us turn our thought to the blessings that do not fade. There is a saying that "All that goes up must come down." It is true in the material world. If values are inflated, they must be deflated; if prices are too high, they must come down. But the man who lives by Spiritual Law is unaffected by these cataclysmic changes. Centering his thought in God's unchanging goodness, he establishes in his consciousness a balance that protects him against all financial storms.

In Spirit, there are no hard times or good times. There is only a steady balance between income and outgo. The man who realizes this truth will not be thrown off his base during good times nor lose his balance during hard times. Knowing that God is everywhere equally present, he will be unaffected by peak or depression, loss or gain, and his income will never wane.

"GOD HATH NOT GIVEN US A SPIRIT OF FEAR, BUT OF LOVE AND POWER, AND OF A SOUND MIND."

44. PROSPERITY AND WORRY

"SEE THAT YE BE NOT TROUBLED."

What warning is Jesus giving us in this text? He is warning us against worry. He wants us to meet the future in an attitude of confidence and faith instead of an attitude of fear and doubt.

Dr. Alexis Carrel said, "Business men who do not know how to fight worry die young." And so do stenographers, bookkeepers, clerks, carpenters, and truck drivers. Young or old, wise or ignorant, rich or poor, religious or irreligious, everybody worries about something; and everybody reaps the harvest of physical and emotional disturbances that worry brings. Dr. Joseph Montague says: "You do not get stomach ulcers from what you eat. You get stomach ulcers from what is eating you."

We worry about things present and about things to come. We worry about yesterday, today, and tomorrow. We worry about our finances and about our business. We worry about the children and their future. We worry about our health, about our souls, and about growing old. In fact, our whole lives are involved in worry and affected by it.

That is why this warning is so timely and practical. Worry is not only one of the most dangerous and harmful emotions, but it is also one of the most costly. It not only greases a man's life toward decay and failure but toward the cemetery. We have all done a lot of foolish things in our life time, but the most foolish thing any one of us ever did was to worry. If you do not believe this, turn to the files of some of America's most prominent physicians. They will tell you that worry is not only the cause of more stomach ulcers, high blood pressure, heart trouble, nervous and digestive disorders, skin eruptions, rheumatism, and arthritis than any other one thing, but also that there is no disease that it does not aggravate.

It may help us in overcoming this useless and harmful habit to realize that the chronic worrier is not born but made. The capacity to worry was not born in us; we acquired it. We learned how to worry. Worry is an achievement. To be a good worrier one must work at it; he must practice. Having practiced, consciously or unconsciously. we face the presence of a habit that must be unlearned. How do we get rid of a worry-thought? By thinking about something else. We replace a troublesome emotion with a pleasant one. Do you know how to do that? Then let us make an experiment right now. Lay the book down, close your eyes, and try to think of the Grand Canyon of Arizona and the thing you are worrying about at the same time. You can't do it, can you? You can think about the Grand Canyon, or you can think about your worry, but you cannot think about both at the same time.

We cannot be worried and peaceful at the same time because negative and positive emotions cannot dwell together at the same time in the same place. One or the other is displaced. That marvelous discovery in the field of psychiatry makes you master of your thought. If you will follow it, there is no bad habit that you cannot overcome. "Reduce your worries," says one of America's foremost salesmen, "and you will double your income." In reducing worry, you will not only direct your thoughts out of worry channels but you replace them with something better. Jesus is not advocating a blind Pollyannaish optimism in this text, but is urging upon us the necessity of keeping our thoughts and emotions true. The great antidote for worry is an active Consciousness of the Presence of God.

"AND THE GOVERNMENT SHALL BE UPON HIS SHOULDERS."

45. PROSPERITY AND XMAS

(Christmas)

"THERE ARE DIVERSITIES OF GIFTS BUT THE SAME SPIRIT."

Why do we introduce the Festival of Christmas in a book on prosperity? Why do we direct your thought to the birth of Jesus Christ? Because that birth is a symbolical pattern of the Creative Process in the individual. It is a step-by-step process of calling forth material and spiritual blessings. We do not have the space here to analyze all the symbols in the Christmas story, but we want to call your attention to two. The Gospel of St. Luke tells us that the Holy Spirit overshadowed Mary (soul), and she magnified the Lord. What does this mean metaphysically? It means that what we magnify (dwell upon) in our subconscious minds becomes manifest in our affairs.

The other symbolism is concerned with the Wise Men of the East. In the Bible, the East symbolizes Heaven – the within, or source of all our good. The West symbolizes the without (the material or relative world). The North symbolizes the Spirit, and the West the manifestation, or form. We turn to the East in our public worship services in the church because it represents all there is. All the desirable and worthwhile things in our lives have come from within; it is to that realm that we must turn to change our circumstances and to demonstrate our supply. Creation is finished; it is here now ready to take form. That is why we must orient ourselves to that inner world. In fact, there is nothing good that can come to us that can compensate for lack of Christ Consciousness.

"Though Christ a thousand times in Bethlehem be born,

If He be not born in you, it is all forlorn."

If we have Him, we do not need anything else. We can say what Emerson said when he was told that the world was coming to an end: "Well, I can do without it." Do you see why a man is not rich until he is independent of material things? To dominate (get dominion over a thing), you must get above it. Just as the Babe of Bethlehem grew up and fulfilled Himself, so your Consciousness of Christ in you must enlarge so that you may fulfill yourself.

Do you remember how the prophets kept the promise of the coming Messiah alive in the hearts of the Hebrews for so many years before His appearance on the earth? They did it by repeated affirmations of their own faith: *"The desire of all nations shall come." "The government shall be upon His shoulder: and His name shall be called Wonderful, Counsellor, The mighty God, The everlasting Father, The Prince of Peace. Of the increase of his government and peace there shall be no end."*

If you were asked to name the law involved here, what would you say? That's right. It is a mental law. "Any idea held in thought, longed for emotionally with constant expectancy, is bound to manifest in the visible, whether it be the idea of an individual or a nation."

"God so loved the world that He gave His only begotten Son." Christmas is primarily a season of giving and receiving following the pattern set by that great gift. Now consider for a moment the gifts that Christ offers to those who recognize them and prepare to receive them.

What is the inmost desire of your heart? Is it a better job? *"Ask, and ye shall receive."* Take your desire into Consciousness and hold it with constant expectancy. Magnify it in your mind. Do not ask God to give you the supervisor's desk or any other specific job. Rather pray, "God, send me that job which is for my highest good." Then act as though your desire had already been fulfilled. If your present job is irksome and distasteful, make your agreement with it. Give it the best you have. In other words, get your release through performance.

Is your desire for greater health? *"Ask, and ye shall receive."* Take your intention into the Silence and hold it with fixity of vision. Stop feeling your ailment, and feel after God. Christ is not a helpless Babe in a cradle in Bethlehem. He is a Living Force. He is the active, responsive Intelligence of the Universe in your own heart. He is there with all the vitality, power, strength, and wholeness which you will ever need. His Presence is powerful enough to penetrate and dispel every inharmonious condition. Do not ask Him to heal a particular ailment or disease; but opening your consciousness to the mighty, cleansing tide of His Spirit, ask Him to wash you clean. The greatest gift is the gift of His Son. Let Him be born in you by right thinking, right acting, and right feeling.

Is your desire for greater prosperity? *"Ask, and ye shall receive."* Do you need more money? Do you need a car? Know that your desire is spiritually legal. Jesus promised us homes, food, clothing, wisdom, power, in the Name of God. Stop feeling your lack and want, and feel the opulence and bounty of God. Believe that you have received. Stop depending upon your salary check, alimony, rent, pension, coupons, or friends. Pray the Lord's Prayer; feel what you say. Look to the East. Listen to the angelic voices. Follow the star. Magnify the Lord in your soul. When you pray, say: *"Give us this day our daily bread."* Bethlehem is the house of bread. It symbolizes everything in God's Kingdom. Stop feeling your debt and lack, and accept your freedom. Release everything in your life that is unlike God; then the Christ Child will come in.

Are you following the star? Can you go all the way with the Wise Men? Then hold your desire with constant expectancy, and it will manifest in the visible. *"And the Word was made flesh, and dwelt among us."*

"GOD DOES NOT BRING TO BIRTH AND NOT BRING
FORTH."

46. PROSPERITY AND YOU

"Use your hidden forces. Do not miss

The purpose of this life, and do not wait

For circumstance to mold or change your fate.

In your own self lies destiny. Let this

Vast truth cast out all fear, all prejudice,

All hesitation. Know that you are great,

Great with divinity. So dominate

Environment, and enter into bliss.

Love largely and hate nothing. Hold no aim

That does not chord with Universal good.

Hear what the voices of the silence say.

All joys are yours if you put forth your claim.

Once let the spiritual laws be understood,

Material things must answer and obey."

In the poem, *Attainment,* Ella Wheeler Wilcox has pointed out the work you must do if you would fulfill your destiny and demonstrate your dominion. Read the poem again, and let me ask you these questions: Are you using your hidden You? Do you have a purpose in life? Are you looking to God to change your fate? Have you cast out all fear, all prejudice, and all hesitation? Do you know that the You of you is great? Do you dominate your environment? Do you love largely and hate nothing? Do you hold any aim that is not in accord with Universal good? Do you understand spiritual laws? If you can answer these questions in the affirmative, material things will come in answer to your call.

In every person there are two yous – the higher You and the lower you, the big You and the little you, the You of you and the you of John Doe; the man who learns to coordinate these Yous is the one who meets success on every plane. When you recognize this You of you and lift it up, everything on the material plane rises up to meet you. Everything in your world begins to improve and you attract only the best from everything and everybody. You cannot, on the other hand, expect to get great results through purely human means.

Why is it necessary to coordinate the little you with the big You? The little you unaided by the big You will accomplish very little. Emerson said, "I, the imperfect, adore my own perfection." Now do you see why St. Paul said, *"I can do all things through Christ* [the Higher You] *which strengtheneth me"?* The big You represents all the Life. Power, Substance, Intelligence, and Supply in the whole universe. Then how does the higher potential flow into the lower so that it can work harmoniously and efficiently on the outer plane? By bringing God Power and man power together. You must not only know the truth, but you must become a humble and perfect instrument through which the Christ can work. In other words, you must use what you have. You must provide ways for the imprisoned splendor to get out.

Let us suppose that someone has left you a large inheritance. What is the first thing you would do? You would go to the attorney who is handling the estate and put in your claim. Would you stop there? No. You would get all the facts and information necessary to back up your claim. Now let us suppose that you did not present the evidence of your right to share in the estate. Could you expect to receive any of the money? You certainly could not.

What are we trying to bring out in this illustration? Simply this: It is using the Truth that brings results. Many students of metaphysics have the mistaken idea that their demonstration begins and ends with reading and studying Truth. They forget that *"Faith without works is dead."* They actually expect to demonstrate prosperity just by reading, studying, and talking Truth. They are like the man who buys a bar bell to exercise, increase, and strengthen his muscles but who never goes any further than reading the instructions.

Jesus said, *"If ye know these things, happy are ye if ye do them."* Why didn't He say, "Happy are ye if ye know these things"? Because knowledge without action is dead. If you do not put your knowledge to work (use it), it cannot accomplish anything for you. If you expect your prosperity to manifest, you must do something more than study and read. You must use your knowledge by acting it out. *"Be ye doers of the word, and not hearers only, deceiving your own selves."*

Understanding, like a muscle, increases with use. The

more you use it the more you have. That is why problems are interesting. They help you to apply your knowledge and to prove the Law. If it were not for your problems, you would vegetate. You would have no way of using or applying the Truth. If you do not believe this, watch the men who retire from business. When they no longer have actual problems to solve, they create imaginary ones and die. It is obvious that the world needs your performance even more than it needs your knowledge.

Now read the poem again, and resolve that you will use it as a measuring stick to prove your divinity and understanding. Let your motto be VICTORY THROUGH PERFORMANCE.

> *"I CONSCIOUSLY BRING ALL THE FORCES OF MY BEING INTO OBEDIENCE TO THE LAW. I ACCEPT MY RESPONSIBILITY AS A CHOSEN INSTRUMENT. I ACT FEARLESSLY, KNOWING THAT IT IS 'THE FATHER THAT DWELLETH IN ME WHO DOETH THE WORKS.' I ACCEPT MY HERITAGE OF DOMINION AND POWER WITH JOY AND THANKSGIVING. I RELY UPON THE PROMISE OF ST. PAUL: 'SIN SHALL NOT HAVE DOMINION OVER YOU.'"*

47. PROSPERITY AND ZEAL

"THE ZEAL OF THY HOUSE HATH EATEN ME UP."

Webster defines zeal as "ardor in pursuit of anything; eagerness, as for a cause; ardent and active interest; enthusiasm; fervor."

If you study the people who call themselves failures, you will find that they have one thing in common – apathy. They have allowed the enthusiasm, fervor, and zeal to go out of their lives. They have lost the quality that makes them useful, effective, and successful, and Life has begun to eliminate them.

Enthusiasm more nearly expresses the nature and activity of God than any other word. If a man has it, he is positive in his attitude. If he doesn't have it, he is negative. The Universe is alive, vibrant, pulsating, abounding, joyous, and advancing. Do you get the feeling of that? The word, *enthusiasm,* comes from two Greek words *en* and *theos* that mean *in God.* It is that something in a man's nature which makes him attractive, dynamic, and effective. It is the Divine Spark that he shares with God. It came with him by virtue of his creation in the Divine Image; it will stay with him as long as he nourishes it in his thought.

But why is zeal so important in the matter of demonstrating prosperity? Because it is that quality in a man's consciousness that keeps him receptive to his good. The zealous man is the prosperous, popular, prominent, sought-after man. Life in him is strong, vibrant, buoyant, and compelling. He radiates power that not only sweeps barrier and obstacles before him but attracts every good thing into his life. *"The zeal of thy house hath eaten me up."* Zeal is an all-consuming thing. The zealous man is an instrument through which the Divine Fire expresses itself in terms of fulfillment. Life to him means but one thing – growth.

It is thrilling to see the zealous man at work. He is like a mighty river flowing out into every area of human need. No matter how commonplace his job may be, he makes it important. No matter how hard times are, he succeeds. He believes in himself and in what he is doing. If he has a quota to meet, he goes over it. If there is a prize for meritorious service, he wins it. Believing in men, he sways and influences them.

ACKNOWLEDGEMENTS

In the making of a book such as this, the author finds himself under obligation to many persons. There are those who have contributed ideas, and there are others whose words are remembered when their source is forgotten or impossible to identify. The appreciation of the writer is no less sincere because of the impossibility of making public acknowledgement of their service.

In the brief bibliography that follows, the author wishes to acknowledge with deep gratitude his use of specific quotations of some length.

1. Williams, Vivian May. *There's Nothing But God.* DeVorss & Co.

4. Ingraham, E. V. *Wells of Abundance.* DeVorss & Co.

5. Beals, Edward C. *Law of Financial Success.* DeVorss & Co.

7. Fillmore, Charles. *Prosperity.* Unity School of Christianity.

8. Lathem, Maude Allison. *Meditations* on *Science of Mind.* Institute of Religious Science.

24. Holmes, Ernest. *The Science of Mind.* Institute of Religious Science.

30. Robinson, Elsie. *Weekly Unity.* Unity School of Christianity.

31. Cliffe, Albert. *Sign Posts.*

38. Gilbert, Charles E. "Income Tax Blessing." *Good Business.* Unity School of Christianity.

39. Wattles, Wallace D. *Financial Success Through Creative Mind.* Elizabeth Towne Co. Inc.

40. Wilcox, Ella Wheeler. "Attainment". *Poems of Power.* W. B. Conkey & Co.

Made in the USA
Columbia, SC
29 March 2024

33783923R00098